Great Ships in New York Harbor

175 HISTORIC PHOTOGRAPHS
1935–2005

William H. Miller, Jr.

DOVER PUBLICATIONS, INC.
Mineola, New York

For Captain Jim McNamara
Marine Master, Historian & Friend
Man of Immense Shipping Knowledge

Bibliographical Note

Great Ships in New York Harbor: 175 Historic Photographs, 1935–2005 is a new work, first published by Dover Publications, Inc., in 2005.

International Standard Book Number: 0-486-44609-3

Book design by Carol Belanger Grafton

Manufactured in the United States of America
Dover Publications, Inc., 31 East 2nd Street, Mineola, N.Y. 11501

Foreword

New York harbor in post–World War II years was one of the most exciting places on earth. The harbor provided the necessary geography to make it the world's premier seaport. It was a time when steam-powered engines were enjoying their last glorious years. Although the diesel engine had made its entry into industry, steam was still the main source of power for railroads, ferries, tramp steamers, colliers, cargo ships, passenger liners, tankers, floating grain elevators, floating cranes, dredges, fishing boats, pilot boats, naval ships, and Coast Guard cutters. This was a time that on any day two or three hundred ships were at their berths in the harbor. Hundreds of tugboats plied their trade, pushing the thousands of barges around the port, as well as assisting ships.

The port served as the major employer of the region. Ships and boats of all descriptions were designed, built, and even scrapped there. They were also chartered, surveyed, positioned, and repaired at the port. And they were prosecuted and defended by the numerous local admiralty law firms. The seafarers required to man the vessels were trained at a number of New York schools: the floating high school *John W. Brown*, the Seamen's Church Institute, New York Maritime College at Fort Schuyler, and, of course, Kings Point, the U.S. Merchant Marine Academy. And the seafarers were cared for and retired at many local institutions including Sailors' Snug Harbor on Staten Island. Truly, New York was experiencing its most glorious days.

My first impression of the port was around 1946. Growing up in Lyndhurst, New Jersey, literally between the Erie Railroad's main line and Lackawanna's Boonton Line, made the five-mile trip to New York City quite easy. As Mondays were always "wash days" at home, my Grandmother would take me on the train to Hoboken, or Jersey City, where we would board a ferryboat and spend the day riding back and forth across the Hudson River. Around lunchtime, we would go ashore in Manhattan and either head north or south along West Street. If we headed south, we would pass the piers of the Belgian Line. When walking by their piers, one could smell the bales of cinnamon, or bags of pepper, which had just arrived from the Belgian Congo or other West African ports. There were also large crates of machinery resting on the cobble streets awaiting shipment. Chain-driven Mack trucks with solid rubber tires would clatter under the elevated West Side Highway. Going further south, you would come to the United Fruit piers across from 17 Battery Place. We were always thrilled to see either the *Chiriqui* or the *Jamaica*, their two U.S.-flag passenger ships, which would be loading, or discharging, their cargoes and passengers from Cuba and Central America. Then in the slip just north of Pier A, about eight to twelve tugboats would gather, with steam up, awaiting orders from their dispatchers who were in offices across the street. The smells and sounds of the steam engines one can never forget.

Fascinated by the port throughout my youth, spare time found me by the piers or on ships with friends and my brother Jay. When I was in the seventh grade, I helped out at the Marine Museum of the Seamen's Church Institute located at 25 South Street. Each year, the old curator, Ralph E. Cropley, was invited aboard the passenger liner *United States* for the overnight voyage to her annual dry-docking at her birthplace, Newport News in Virginia. He was allowed to take along one guest, and asked my parents to allow me to go. On December 19, 1958, at eight o'clock in the evening, I began my seagoing career. The great ship was practically empty as we sailed that night. There were no passengers, only about twenty guests of the owners, the United States Lines, and myself. It was during this 15-hour trip that I decided on my future: I would go to sea.

Although many excellent books have been written about "maritime New York," very few have been able to capture the feel of its busiest era, which is now, sadly, past. Most of what has been so eloquently described and illustrated in this book has disappeared. One cannot smell the pepper and cinnamon, for example, as these cargoes are now shipped in freight containers. Parents and children can no longer wander around the piers, having easy access to the ships. No longer does a tugboat captain invite an interested tourist to come aboard. It is a far different world today. Then, after September 11, 2001, still more changes occurred, but for quite a different reason. On July 1, 2004, the International Ship & Port Facility Security Code (ISPS) and the Maritime Transportation Security Act (MTSA) was implemented. These two laws literally fenced-off all U.S. seaports from the eye of the public for reasons of security.

Together, these events make this book of Bill's even more valuable. It would be difficult, if not impossible, to capture the activity and excitement of the New York waterfront and tell the story as Bill has done. I expect this book to be a "must have," not only for ship buffs and those of us who experienced those times, but for all those interested in our city, as well as historians of the future. Nice work, Bill!

CAPTAIN JAMES MCNAMARA
New York City
August 2004

Captain McNamara, president of the National Cargo Bureau, served for many years aboard the freighters of the States Marine Lines. He is also famous within the maritime industry for having a photographic memory of names, tonnage, and ownership of virtually every ship he has ever seen. Moreover, he knows the litany of changed names and owners for each vessel, from launching to scrapping. He also knows as much as anyone about the peculiarities of New York harbor.

Acknowledgments

Just as there was a huge cast—the crews, the dockers, the shipyard workers, the floating crane operators, the firefighters onboard the fireboats, and the narrators on the Circle Line, there was also a good-size cast that assisted me in the organization, creation, and final production of this photo-filled book. It has been a pleasure voyage for me of pure nostalgia.

First of all, my greatest appreciation and respect for the splendid Dover Publications. They have had ongoing, undiminished interest and enthusiasm for maritime titles over the past 25 years, beginning in 1979 from my first meetings with the late Hayward Cirker and his expert staff at Dover's Varick Street offices. Mr. Cirker was a tireless promoter, inspiration, and the greatest of instigators for these nautical picture books. In particular, he so enjoyed documenting all aspects of history, life, and the ongoing human process. Fortunately, based on his young days on Atlantic crossings, he was fascinated by passenger ships. These days, at Dover, I am deeply indebted to some of his successors: Clarence Strowbridge, for taking these titles on; Suzanne E. Johnson, for her editorial skills and sense of accuracy and detail; and to Carol Belanger Grafton, for her flawless design and layout.

Away from Dover itself, the "crew" that provides photos, information, and the smallest of helpful details begins with a first-class group that includes Ernest Arroyo, Frank Braynard, Kitty Carlisle Hart, Tom Cassidy, the late Frank Cronican, Captain Dag Dvergastein, Richard Faber, the late John Gillespie, Norman Knebel, Captain James McNamara, Richard Morse, Sal Scannella, Jane Bouche Strong, and Commodore Ronald Warwick. They are never reluctant, or hesitant, to loan that prized picture, share their knowledge, or provide some other element of support and assistance. Highest praises to Abe Michaelson, my business partner, who promotes, sells, and distributes books such as these to all the seven seas. I would also like to extend my warmest thanks to Anthony Cooke, Luis Miguel Correia, Maurizio Eliseo, James Flood, James Giammatteo, the late Jacob Goldstein, Andy Hernandez, the late Captain Fred Johnson, Arnold Kludas, Peter Lancaric, Stan Lehrer, Victor Marinelli, the late Captain Joseph Mazzotta, Hisashi Noma, Harold Oshzy, Robert Pelletier, Paolo Piccione, Fred Rodriguez, Rich Romano, the late Victor Scrivens, Captain Ed Squire, Gordon Turner, Jack Watson, and Al Wilhelmi. There's also need to mention Frank Andrews, Tom Chirby, and Steve Cryan.

Firms and organizations that greatly assisted include Alcoa Steamship Company, Carmania Press Limited, Carnival Cruise Lines, Celebrity Cruises, Crystal Cruises, Cunard Line, Hoboken Museum & Historical Society, Moran Towing & Transportation Company, the Ocean Liner Council at the South Street Seaport Museum, Port Authority of New York & New Jersey, Radisson–Seven Seas Cruises, Sea-Land Corporation, Steamship Historical Society (especially the Long Island Chapter), World Ocean & Cruise Society, and the World Ship Society. There are also those companies which are, alas, no more, such as American Export Lines, Bethlehem Steel Company, Erie Railroad, Flying Camera, Inc., and the French Line. If I have failed to mention anyone else, my great apologies. But know that you are all well appreciated and have assisted in keeping a part of our maritime history alive.

Introduction

It is just before five o'clock in the morning. The panoramic view from the bridge of the world's largest ocean liner, the *Queen Mary 2*, is both bewildering and extraordinary. We are still over an hour from the Verrazano-Narrows Bridge, from the official entrance of New York harbor, and therefore, according to calculations, two hours from tying up at Pier 92, at the foot of 52nd Street, on Manhattan's West Side. The view ahead is one of deep black, that lonely, sometimes frightening, but certainly endless abyss that nighttime creates. There are a few pinhead lights off in the distance, those to the east representing Long Island and possibly Brooklyn, and those on the left being New Jersey. The 4,260-foot-wide bridge is itself almost completely dark, which adds to the mysterious tone. Commodore Ronald Warwick, the master of the 148,000-ton supership, has been up for hours, and so have most of his young, white-suited juniors. They offer me a cup of coffee, an urgent, most necessary tonic in those hours long before those multicoursed, shipboard breakfasts begin. A pilot, in suit and tie, has joined us as well, having come aboard from a launch just minutes before and then escorted in a speedy elevator to the bridge. There are the customary cordial greetings, done the way that two kings might if sharing the same castle. More or less, captain and pilot are equals. Below, of course, many of the staff are already at work, especially the armies of luggage handlers, looking after some 5,500 pieces in all that will be off-loaded at Pier 92.

The *Queen Mary 2* is moving at a brisk 18 knots, down from the 28 she was averaging on our 6-day, 3,400-mile passage westwards from Southampton, England. The 62-year-old Commodore, the son, in fact, of Commodore William Warwick, the first master of the *Mary's* predecessor, the *Queen Elizabeth 2*, in 1969, feels that arriving in New York is one of sea travel's finest and most memorable occasions. As always, he is quietly, but clearly thrilled. He, too, is fascinated as those pinhead, shoreline lights grow brighter, larger, and more extensive. An outbound containership passes us on the port side, but her few lights make identification all but impossible to me. The Commodore, the pilot, and the officers know her name, of course, but she seems to be of little consequence other than her being a safe distance away from the 1,132-foot-long Cunard flagship.

At almost precisely five o'clock, with microphone in hand, I will begin a one-hour narration of our arrival into, what is to me, the greatest port in the world. My words will be heard, however, only on the outer, open decks. The narrative is not meant to be an alarm clock to some of the 2,622 passengers residing for their final hours in some 1,310 cabins and suites. Usually, I start when we are about a half-mile before the Verrazano. A distant, rather strange glow, which is far-off Manhattan, reflects above on the low-hanging, early morning clouds. Indeed, it is like approaching Oz. I've done it at least fifty times, sailing into New York harbor by ship that is, but it never fails to excite me. Laced with more than the tinges of sadness at leaving such a superb ship, a moving

"fantasy island," there is the concurrent, mounting excitement of returning home. The longer the trip, the greater the excitement, or so it seems. Combined with the eastbound crossing and a two-week cruise from Southampton to Scandinavia and Northern Europe, this trip on the *Queen Mary 2* for me has lasted 28 days in all.

Those great strands of twinkling lights, a splendid necklace, appear suddenly. It is the Verrazano. Red blinkers are flashing atop the twin, 700-foot-high towers, and the lights of predawn motorists, those daily commuters and inevitable truckers, can be seen moving between the Brooklyn and Staten Island shores. It is our first sign that on this workday the great city and, indeed, the great port are coming to life. We pass under the twin levels of the 40-year-old bridge with just about 14 feet to clear. The Commodore seems not to especially notice. He has been under it dozens of times on his previous command, the *Queen Elizabeth 2*, and maybe a half-dozen times since the *Mary 2's* maiden arrival at New York three months before.

"Being aboard the *Queen Mary 2's* maiden crossing from Southampton to New York last April was very special to me," said the Commodore as he stopped by on a walk over to the far end of the port bridge wing. "It is not just about the sea and about liners, but about being part of the great history of the Cunard Line. Cunard is very special. To me, there is nothing quite like it anywhere. The current Cunard and the QM2 are the links to Samuel Cunard's vision that began back in the late 1830s. There is a great element of heritage. It is an incredible continuation from a small steamer to this 148,000-ton ship, the largest liner yet built. Just as Halifax is important for Cunard's first voyage, the first arrival in New York of a Cunard ship is also very significant and historic. Southampton to New York is also true Cunard. And New York is my favorite port of call. The Verrazano-Narrows Bridge is man-made grandeur. The Statue of Liberty is the ultimate gift from one nation to another, and a gift that became a national symbol. Ellis Island symbolizes a process of humanity, the idea that 'it is good over there,' a concept that inspired and influenced millions. It convinced the Old World to take a chance on the New World and yet to endure appalling conditions en route. The Manhattan skyline is constantly changing. There are always new buildings reaching for the sky as if New York City is still trying to catch up. Overall, there is great shipping history in the Port of New York. You can just imagine it in its heyday. Now, it has new purposes, and that adds to its fascination. There are new symbols, such as the keeling of this ship on July 4, 2002, and the groundbreaking for the Freedom Tower on July 4, 2004."

A half-dozen tankers, some of them rather large, sit at anchorage in the Narrows. They are awaiting berths, inspections, and security clearances. Conditionally, they seem to be extremely well lit, with individual beacons of high-intensity, lemon-yellow light. Historically, it was here that the great liners, particularly in pre-1914 times, paused on their inbound voyages and, with a ferry, tender, or barge alongside, off-loaded all of their third-class and steerage passengers. These low-fare voyagers were arriving in New York, in the New World, for the very first time, where "the streets were said to be paved with gold," but they were not permitted the luxury, or convenience, of admittance through the port's piers and terminals. Instead, they had to go to Ellis Island for dreaded inspections, intimidating interrogations, and fearful examinations. It was here that the great convoys of the Second World War gathered before setting off for Murmansk, the Normandy beaches, and North Africa. The newest of ships, especially the great liners, also appeared here for the first time on their maiden calls and, like chicks about a mother hen, were surrounded and serenaded by a flotilla of smaller welcoming craft: the tugs, charter boats, spraying fireboats, and pleasure craft. Otherwise, a few tugs seemed to be off on early assignments, and the first of the Staten Island ferries, with twin rows of glowing windows, was setting off on its 20-minute commuter run to Whitehall in Lower Manhattan. I emphasize in my narrative that it is the "best short ocean ride in the world."

Passengers are now crowding the outer decks, cameras of all sorts in hand. The early morning charcoal-colored sky gives way, in the east at least, over still, sleepy Brooklyn, to a slight pink that becomes a sort of cantaloupe color. High-riding, empty oil barges wait in the Lower Bay, the muscular tugs at their sterns being much like the nanny, the nursemaid, to the child at sleep.

As the early day's sky brightens, the majestic Statue of Liberty remains lighted, her torch and crown so easily identified. Even new arrivals to New York harbor know her and some non-Americans actually seem to be the keenest, most excited, and passionate of all. Just beyond are the four towers of Ellis Island, which is now a successful museum and tribute to that great age of immigration, indeed the Golden Door to America. Some eighteen million people passed through its corridors, halls, and waiting rooms. If it were not for the rigidly timed schedule, the QM2 would almost certainly pause there in courteous homage, a sort of deep curtsey to two of the greatest American symbols. But cameras are barely given a rest when, on the starboard side, the soaring, clustered, castle-like skyline of Lower Manhattan comes into full view. We have just about reached Oz.

Those great towers seem to fight with one another in their reach for the heavens, indeed the mighty symbols of Yankee corporate might. Wall Street, that name synonymous with high finance, is surrounded within, almost guarded by, its skyscraper soldiers. The huge, long stretches of landfill, now called Battery City and lined with luxury high-rises and office towers, has long since replaced the first of those steamship finger piers that once lined the bustling shores of Manhattan Island. In my youth, some fifty years before, here were the busy, almost hectic piers that belonged to the likes of United Fruit, the Belgian Line, Alcoa, and the Venezuelan Lines. Onward, the bulky towers of the World Financial Center mark the site, just behind, of Ground Zero, where the World Trade Center's twin towers stood for some thirty years.

In the Hudson, or more precisely the North River to navigators and seamen, purposeful ferries began their relays, assembling at awakening docks in Jersey City, Hoboken, and Weehawken. The great stage production that is today's Port of New York is coming to life, a maritime drama beginning with Act I. Further along, most of the piers, docks, and warehouses along both sides of the river are now gone, or at least replaced by parklands, offices, and expensive apartments. Big plants like Jersey City's Colgate-Palmolive and Hoboken's Maxwell House have fallen victim to the wrecking ball, replaced by towers filled with stockbrokers, and roomy apartments with trendy professionals. Indeed, the harborscape has changed enormously, but it is renewed, redeveloping, and growing forcefully. And unlike earlier times, ordinary people flock to the waterfront these days.

The 17-deck-high *Queen Mary 2* has slowed by the time she is off Chelsea, those docks around West 20th Street now used for recreation, restaurants, and television production, which once welcomed an earlier generation of Atlantic ocean liners. On a summer's morning of, say, seventy years ago, long before speedy airline connections, one might see grand ships like the *Manhattan, Britannic, Rex, Ile de France, Majestic,* and *Aquitania*. Dozens of raked funnels would have rested atop the pier sheds, well-known symbols of that bygone, working Manhattan waterfront. Midtown, another grand conglomeration of towers, dominated by the beloved Empire State Building, hints that the city is very close, nearly upon us. Carefully, the *Mary* moves to those three piers that once were part of Luxury Liner Row, specially created in the 1930s for an evolutionary larger and longer group of ocean liners, grand ships like the *Normandie* and the *Queen Mary 2*. Those ships sometimes used a dozen tugs. With her high-precision maneuverability, the mammoth, new Cunarder needs only one, or sometimes two, tugboats. Quickly, the docking lines are secured—the great ship is officially and determinedly in the great port. The well-orchestrated process has little variation. Everyone, it seems, has a task. And now, of course, the journey is complete. Breakfast, farewells, that call to disembarkation, the collection of luggage, and then homeward.

I have lived in and around New York harbor all of my life. It has been an ongoing love affair. The port has changed enormously, but many changes have been for the better, including improvements and modifications that have paralleled the overall progress and evolution. There has been the shift in cargo-handling from break-bulk to more efficient container, for example, which, more than anything else, has altered the landscape of the harbor. The introduction of jet travel nearly killed off the transatlantic passenger ship business, but, for the most part, ocean liners have gloriously reinvented themselves as leisurely cruise ships. Statistically, the port still has prominence. In fact, more cargo is being handled at New York than any other U.S. East Coast port, and more passengers are traveling by liner than at any time in the past forty years. In many ways, it is business as usual.

But there is always a need for a look back, a voyage of nostalgia, a steamboat excursion down memory lane. I began this photo-filled journey in 1935, the year when there were one hundred active shipping piers jutting out from Manhattan, 400 tugs serving an endless armada of oceangoing ships that traded to the farthest corners of the earth, and of the immortal, innovative, thoroughly magnificent *Normandie*'s gala maiden arrival. She is often said to have been the greatest ocean liner of them all. The ensuing years are, I think, very interesting as well. There are many more liners and freighters, tugs, ferryboats, terminals, and shipyards. The whistles are sounding—so let us begin our voyage around the great Port of New York.

BILL MILLER
Secaucus, New Jersey
Fall 2004

Contents

Photo Credits

Alcoa Steamship Company: page 15 (bottom)

Ernest Arroyo Collection: pages 89 (bottom), 90 (all), 91 (top)

Author's Collection: pages 7, 8 (all), 9 (bottom), 10 (top), 15 (top), 18 (top), 40 (top), 42 (bottom), 48 (bottom), 58 (top)

Frank O. Braynard Collection: pages 11 (top), 18 (bottom), 19 (top), 22 (top), 30 (bottom), 52 (bottom), 54 (top), 61 (top), 62 (bottom), 64 (top), 66 (bottom), 68 (bottom), 70 (bottom), 91 (bottom)

Carnival Cruise Lines: page 97 (bottom)

Cronican-Arroyo Collection: pages 3 (top), 34 (bottom), 35 (bottom), 36 (top), 37 (all), 39 (bottom), 44 (top left, bottom left), 45, 47 (bottom), 48 (middle), 49, 53 (top), 63 (bottom), 67, 70 (top), 72 (bottom), 75 (all), 78 (top), 79 (bottom), 81 (top), 82 (all), 83 (all), 84 (all), 85 (all), 87 (all), 88 (all), 89 (top)

Cunard Line: pages 39 (top right), 40 (bottom), 42 (top), 96 (top), 98

Erie Railroad: page 65 (top)

Richard Faber Collection: pages 33 (bottom), 34 (top), 38 (top), 39 (top left), 41 (left), 41 (bottom right), 50 (all), 80, 81 (bottom)

Flying Camera, Inc.: pages 9 (top), 25 (bottom), 55 (bottom), 73 (bottom)

French Line: pages 35 (top), 36 (bottom)

James Giammatteo Collection: page 58 (bottom)

Gillespie-Faber Collection: pages 2 (all), 16 (top), 17, 20 (bottom), 21 (all), 22 (bottom), 23 (all), 24 (all), 25 (top), 28 (bottom), 30 (top), 47 (top), 48 (top), 56 (all), 57 (top), 60 (top), 63 (top), 66 (middle), 71 (all), 73 (top), 76 (bottom), 79 (top), 93, 94 (bottom), 95 (all), 97 (top)

Norman Knebel Collection: pages 3 (bottom), 53 (bottom), 54 (bottom)

Peter Lancaric Collection: pages 16 (bottom), 27 (bottom)

James McNamara Collection: pages 4 (bottom), 6 (bottom), 11 (bottom), 12, 13 (top), 26 (top), 27 (top), 33 (top), 51 (bottom), 55 (top), 66 (top), 86 (bottom)

Moran Towing & Transportation Company: pages 5, 10 (bottom), 26 (bottom), 28 (top), 31, 38 (bottom), 44 (top right), 44 (bottom right), 51 (top), 61 (bottom), 64 (bottom), 65 (bottom), 72 (top), 76 (top)

Robert Pelletier Collection: page 68 (top)

Port Authority of New York & New Jersey: frontispiece, pages 4 (top), 6 (top), 13 (bottom), 20 (top), 29 (all), 43 (top), 57 (bottom), 60 (bottom), 62 (top), 74

Fred Rodriguez Collection: page 96 (bottom)

Sal Scannella Collection: pages 19 (bottom), 41 (middle right)

Victor Scrivens Collection: page 78 (bottom)

Sea-Land Corporation: page 94 (top)

United States Lines: pages 41 (top right), 43 (bottom)

Al Wilhelmi Collection: pages 46 (all), 52 (top)

World Ship Society: page 86 (top)

CHAPTER ONE
The Great Port: The Vast Docklands

"New York harbor was the greatest place in the world to me," recalled the late Jacob Goldstein, a Manhattan native and keen maritime enthusiast. He began visiting the waterfront in the 1930s and continued for some sixty years. "The harbor was one of the busiest places in the city. There was always activity: the big liners, freighters, ferries, tugs, and barges. And it had its own symphony: the sounds of throaty whistles from the great passenger ships, lesser tones from the freighters, screeches from the tugboats and ferries and, in ways most enchanting of all, the chorus of fog horns. I would walk along West Street, from the bottom end at Battery Place all the way to the top of Luxury Liner Row at 57th Street. On weekdays and Saturdays as well, there was great life along the piers: the dockers, trucks, the noises of the ships themselves being loaded and unloaded, the excitement of passengers and visitors boarding the liners, and the general sounds of commerce.

"In the late 1930s, as a schoolboy, I knew all the ships that berthed along Manhattan's West Shore. There were the all-white banana boats of United Fruit down at Morris and Rector streets, the little passenger ships of the Eastern Steamship Lines that sailed to Boston and Nova Scotia and sometimes down to Bermuda, and others like the Grace Line, United States Lines, and the Panama Mail Line. I followed the arrivals and departures of the ships daily schedules in the *New York Times* and *Herald Tribune.*"

He continued, "Sometimes I would take one of the Staten Island ferries just for the ride back and forth. The outer bay was chockablock with ships, those fascinating, always romantic freighters and tramp steamers and, of course, an endless parade of busy, shuttling, purposeful harborcraft: the tugs, barges, those railroad carfloats. If I was very lucky, great ships like the *Aquitania* or the *Queen Mary* would sweep past, usually outbound and headed off to Europe on another crossing. From those wooden benches of those ferries, it was like being in the movies. There was no better entertainment."

On Saturday mornings, young Goldstein often went uptown, to the piers dubbed Luxury Liner Row. "Those piers were the busiest marine terminals in the world," he said. "Great ocean liners, traveling mostly to and from Europe in those pre-jet days, came and went with almost daily regularity. And there were times, especially in summer, when as many as eight, ten, even twelve of them gathered at the same time. These piers stretched for a dozen city blocks, from Pier 84 at West 44th Street to Pier 97 at West 57th Street. While thousands of passengers passed through the entrances, the docks were a destination within themselves. Many went over to the West Side just to see the great liners and sometimes tour them. And I believe that many like me have nostalgic memories of that now bygone, vanished era."

In 1939, when he was thirteen, Jacob was given twenty-five cents by his father, and a nickel for each way on the subway, to go downtown and see the liners. "There were lots of weekday sailings, but also many on Saturdays. I remember seeing the *Queen Mary, Ile de France, Champlain, Conte di Savoia*, and many others. I especially recall seeing Sara Delano Roosevelt, the President's mother, sail off on the *Conte di Savoia* on a Saturday in 1937. There were lots of security men about. But on that Saturday in 1939, I wanted to see the most fabulous liner of them all, the *Normandie*."

The 83,400-ton *Normandie* was called "the Queen of New York Harbor" and was not only the world's largest liner at the time, but certainly the most luxurious, best fed and served and, perhaps, the most fanciful ship at sea. She was a stunning creation of brilliant artistry, design, and decoration. Her first-class restaurant, for example, was done in bronze, hammered glass, and Lalique, and could seat 1,000 guests at 400 tables. The lavish Winter Garden included fountains, greenery, and exotic birds in cages. There was an outdoor, as well as an illuminated indoor pool, a children's playland, chocolate and flower shops, and a men's shop that could produce a tailored suit within the 5 days it took to reach the French side of the North Atlantic. Every first-class suite and stateroom was done in a different decor and Hollywood films were premiered in the first complete movie theater to go to sea.

"I remember the great activity of those big, yellow Checker-style cabs that steadily came and went in front of Pier 88, the French Line terminal at the very foot of West 48th Street," added Goldstein. "It was very exciting. The *Normandie* was my favorite ship and she was sailing that afternoon. To me, everything about her was special, including the passengers going aboard. She seemed bigger than life! The *Normandie* was so huge that it hung over the street edge of the berth."

Young Goldstein paid a princely ten cents to board the 1,028-foot-long superliner on that Saturday morning. "There was great excitement everywhere, even in the peculiar smells of the Hudson River. It was all so glamorous. To board the *Normandie* was to enter a fantasyland of glass and mirrors, art, and beautiful decor. There seemed to be buckets of fresh flowers, the sounds of popping corks from champagne bottles, and the smell of expensive perfumes, mostly French, of course. I was impressed by everything about the *Normandie* including the posted passenger list. I recognized name after name from the arts & society pages of the newspapers. And many of them were traveling with ten, fifteen, even twenty steamer trunks."

Goldstein's boyhood visits were abruptly curtailed that fall when World War II erupted in Europe, and almost all the foreign-flag ships, including the *Normandie*, ceased their commercial sailings in and out of New York. "I always felt a little depressed when I went ashore," he concluded. "The ships sailed away. That was part of the great romance of New York harbor: the link to far-off, exciting places."

The stoic Ambrose Lightship was long considered a sort of formal entrance to New York harbor. It certainly served as the marker for the great Atlantic steamship races, those quests between ships, shipowners, and whole nations for the coveted Blue Riband. For well over a century, great passenger ships vied with one another for the honor that, along with obvious prestige and notoriety, brought them more passengers and greater profits. The brilliant *United States* was, however, the last of the mighty line of oceangoing speed queens. Sparkling, a great moving symbol of Yankee design, construction, and mechanical genius, she set off from the Ambrose Light on July 3, 1952. She then fulfilled every expectation by crossing to England's Bishop's Rock in 3 days and 10 hours at an average speed of 35.59 knots. But by 1958, great, silver-colored jets would begin flying the Atlantic, instantly bringing passages down from 6 days to 6 hours. In this view *(above)*, dated August 27, 1951, the stately *Ile de France* is inbound, passing the Lightship to the right.

The Narrows is another entry point to the port. It is not at all narrow, of course, and was perhaps best highlighted by the creation of the Verrazano-Narrows Bridge. With two 700-foot-high towers supporting thick cables and twin levels of traffic, the world's largest suspension bridge, as it was for a time, was formally opened in November 1964. In this scene *(below)*, dating from April 1964, construction cranes are still in place and busily at work. The brand-new pride of the Israeli Merchant Navy, the French-built *Shalom*, is arriving on her maiden voyage.

The Lower Bay has long been the setting of vast anchorage for ships: vessels awaiting a berth, requiring added inspection, loading or off-loading cargo into barges or, in the case of tramp steamers, awaiting their next freight, even their next charter. The Lower Bay has also been traditionally the ideal setting for the first glimpse of a new ship, especially the highly publicized ocean liners of the past. In this view *(above)*, dating from June 3, 1935, the splendid French *Normandie*, the world's largest, longest, fastest, and most luxurious passenger ship of her day, arrives for the very first time. Thousands flocked to the shoreline for their first glimpse of this extraordinary vessel.

Ships passed through the Lower Bay with great frequency. In this view *(below)* from the late 1960s, we see an outbound tanker, the *Pasadena*, passing an arriving freighter, Blue Funnel Line's Far East–routed *Priam*. "The *Pasadena* was owned by the American-flag Trinidad Corporation," noted Captain James McNamara. "She was actually a jumbo-sized T2 tanker, built during the Second World War, which sailed until the late 1970s. She and her three sisters sailed the American coastal oil trade, between New York and Houston."

Until the 1960s, summer days often meant great armadas of European-bound Atlantic liners. They would have departed, often minutes apart, from Luxury Liner Row along Manhattan's West Side. In this scene *(opposite, top)*, from the early afternoon of July 12, 1956, there are five liners underway at the same time. The Greek Line's *New York* is in the foreground on the right, French Line's *Flandre* is to the left with Cunard's *Queen Elizabeth*, then the world's largest liner, just behind. Farther behind are Holland America's *Ryndam* and the *Giulio Cesare* of the Italian Line.

Staten Island had its own set of working finger piers: long, slender and often single-story docks that reached out into the Lower Bay. The Stapleton Piers, shown here *(opposite, bottom)* in 1950, were often used by military vessels. Here we see three peacetime troopships awaiting orders: the USS *Pvt. William H. Thomas* is at the far left with the *George W. Goethals* behind her. The larger *General E. T. Collins* is at the outer end.

Early morning often meant that great liners were inbound, expected to moor at their city berths by seven or eight o'clock. With the tower-filled Manhattan skyline resting above, the 25,000-ton *Empress of England*, owned by Britain's Canadian Pacific Steamships, arrives in the port for the first time *(above)*. The date is January 13, 1958, and the 1,058-passenger ship has come from Liverpool for a winter season of cruises from New York to the sunny Caribbean.

The Statue of Liberty is the port's most beloved, cherished, and certainly most symbolic structure. In this midday scene (*opposite, top*), the *Queen Mary* is outbound, passing the very tip of Manhattan Island as she begins yet another 5-day passage to Cherbourg, France and Southampton, England.

The tip of Manhattan Island, marked by the Battery at the very bottom end, was noted for banking and shipping. Until the 1970s, almost all the great steamship companies had offices amidst what was otherwise known as the Financial District. In this aerial view (*opposite, bottom*), from March 1961, dozens of piers jut out into

the Hudson on the left and, while fewer and less famous, others on the right poke out into the East River.

This spectacular aerial photo (*above*), dated 1940, shows the narrowing form of the bottom end of Manhattan Island and the juxtaposition of this lower section of the city to Brooklyn. The East River to the left and the Hudson River on the lower right converge into the Upper Bay (top right.) An Eastern Steamship Lines passenger ship, the *Evangeline*, lies at her Chambers Street pier at the bottom while the Havana-routed cruise ship *Oriente* is at berth at the foot of Wall Street (top left) on the East River.

The Hudson, also known to navigators as the North River, is at its widest at the lower end between Jersey City and Lower Manhattan. In this 1948 view *(above)*, we see American Export Lines' ships berthed in Jersey City's Harborside Terminal, while beyond are other Jersey City and then Hoboken docks. Across the river is the great stretch of busily working piers that stretched from Battery Park north to West 70th Street.

Manhattan and Brooklyn (right) are at the top of this 1965 view *(below)* while Hoboken (left) and Jersey City fill out the lower half.

It seems a quiet winter afternoon in this 1964 view *(above)* overlooking the three piers of the American Export Lines' terminal in Hoboken. Across the river in Manhattan, the cruise ship *Victoria* is berthed at West 10th Street in Greenwich Village. Uninterrupted, Lackawanna Railroad ferries ply their steady runs between Hoboken and Lower Manhattan's Barclay Street.

Looking over Manhattan's Chelsea section, the great West Side piers reach out into the Hudson *(below)*. Jersey City (left) and Hoboken are on the opposite side with the famed New Jersey Meadowlands in the distance beyond.

Luxury Liner Row, the great passenger ship terminals *(above)*, stretched from Pier 84, at the foot of West 44th Street (lower right) north to Pier 97, at West 57th Street (middle left). It was a great destination in itself, especially in the years prior to the 1960s, before the airlines grabbed most of the overseas passenger trades. These docks were known to millions, the starting point of voyages to Europe and the returns as well. In this view from June 1935, the spectacular *Normandie*, arriving for the first time, is being carefully berthed in brand-new Pier 88 at West 48th Street. Five other liners, not as large as the new French flagship, are in port as well: Sweden's *Kungsholm* is at the top left, then the *Monarch of Bermuda* of Furness Bermuda, and the *Cameronia* of the Anchor Line. To the right are two German liners, Hamburg America's *Albert Ballin* and the three-funnel *Resolute*.

The great stretch of the lower Brooklyn waterfront *(below)*

includes the Army Terminal (left), opened in 1919, and then the six piers of the Bush Terminal, a large cargo facility constructed in 1905. Both facilities were demolished, however, by the 1990s. This photo dates from 1971.

The Erie Basin in Brooklyn's Red Hook district was one of the port's busiest cargo ship terminals and included the Todd Shipyard as well. Isthmian Lines, a large freighter company owned by United States Steel, leased the entire outer arm and is seen by their rooftop advertising in this 1951 photo *(opposite, top)*. Manhattan Island is beyond at the top and the docks of Brooklyn Heights above to the right.

The geography of the upper Brooklyn waterfront and Manhattan Island beyond is very clearly seen in this dramatic aerial photo *(opposite, bottom)* dated June 11, 1964.

Deep-sea shipping continued farther along the East River. In this view *(above)*, dated 1960, a Norwegian-flag Meyer Line freighter is off-loading cargo of sugar at Long Island City. The head-quarters of the United Nations, located at the foot of East 42nd Street, can be seen just opposite.

In the distant outer reaches of the port, marine facilities in Newark, New Jersey, located some 15 miles west of New York City, began to expand. Shippers especially appreciated the vast spaces for trucks, which were at an expensive and diminishing premium in the city. The vast docks of what became known as Port Newark can be seen in this 1970s view *(opposite, top)*.

Far above the city, some 40 miles along the Hudson near Haverstraw, New York, were the 200 or so ships that created the U.S. Government Reserve Fleet *(opposite, bottom)*. Mostly World War II cargo ships, they were kept in case of a national emergency, a call that for many of them would never come. There were also several former passenger liners, ships such as the *Washington, Manhattan,* and former *America* of 1905, that sat out their final years in this "dead fleet," which itself was disbanded by the early 1970s.

CHAPTER TWO
Cargo of All Kinds: Those Busy Freighters

In the spring of 2002, demolition crews were busily at work pulling down another part of New York harbor history: Pier 9 in Jersey City. A 1,500-foot-long, green-colored terminal, located just across the mighty lower Hudson from Manhattan's Tribeca and Soho districts, almost directly opposite Canal Street. Amidst the varied buildings and landmarks of New York harbor, it would have been a very ordinary structure except that at the far, outer end stood the yellow brick-faced, New Jersey ventilator tower for the Holland Tunnel. A twin stood at the opposite side, at the far end of old Pier 34, at the foot of Manhattan's Spring Street. Within weeks, Pier 9, an otherwise derelict, unused terminal was flattened. The removal was part of a major upgrading and renewal of properties along both sides of the lower Hudson, areas now dominated by corporate towers, luxury high-rises, townhouse complexes, vast marinas, upscale restaurants, and manicured parklands.

Pier 9 was built in 1929 and, unlike most harbor docks, had a steady tenant for decades: the American President Lines. They were one of some 200 freighter companies that regularly used New York in the 1950s. San Francisco–based APL, as they were also known, was a busy company. Often, there were President ships on both sides of Pier 9. The company ran three distinct services, which in themselves kept the pier very busy. There was a westward around-the-world service, which departed from Jersey City for Havana, the Panama Canal, Mexico, Los Angeles, and San Francisco, and then onward to the Orient, India, the Suez Canal, and home through the Mediterranean. After the Second World War up until 1965 two passenger-cargo ships supported this run: the 9,600-ton, 96-berth *President Monroe* and *President Polk*. Their 100-day voyages were priced from $3,200 (in 1960) and were popular not only with wealthy retirees, but travelers who

preferred the casual atmosphere of such smaller ships rather than the big luxury liner and around-the-world cruise ships. Sleek Mariner class freighters, built in the 1950s and among the largest and fastest cargo vessels of their day (9,600 tons and 20-knot service speeds), assisted on this service. These ships carried large amounts of freight, as well as a dozen passengers. Their quarters were among the finest on any freighter of that era and included wood-paneled staterooms, spacious lounges, and even a passenger elevator.

Another American President service from Jersey City was to the Far East via Panama and Hawaii. World War II–built, C3-type freighters, also with twelve passenger berths, generally ran on this service. Finally, there was an intercoastal service, connecting U.S. East Coast ports to others in California. The company also operated several wartime-built Victory ships, which carried only four passengers each, usually restricted to males only, and all housed in the same four-berth cabin.

High U.S. maritime labor costs gradually reduced the American President fleet in the 1960s. (Since the 1980s, American President has been owned by Singapore-headquartered Neptune Orient Lines.) The company moved to more spacious cargo facilities at Port Newark, New Jersey, in 1970. Helsinki-based Finnlines leased Pier 9 for a short time before it was shut down completely. By the late '80s, there were plans to restore the facility as a Jacques Cousteau Undersea Research Museum as part of the developing Newport City high-rise and shopping mall development project just streets away. The museum idea never came to pass, and a small fire later destroyed part of the outer end of the dock. Its fate was sealed. Although it took a few more years before demolition crews arrived to start their work.

The long stretch of piers along Manhattan's West Side began with a large sign that read "The Great White Fleet—United Fruit." Fruitco, as it was also known, was synonymous with all-white banana boats that sailed to romantic tropics like Cuba, Jamaica, and ports in Central America. With its offices uniquely located on Pier 3, at the foot of Morris Street, United Fruit leased four docks in all, and were known to have as many sailings each week, three of them often on Friday afternoons. In this 1950 view *(above)*, we see four ships in port: the three vessels to the left, each wearing a distinctive white diamond on their funnels, are owned by United Fruit under the American flag, while the ship to the right is on charter and is of foreign registry. "This wonderful view of those once busy United Fruit piers at the bottom end of West Street includes the *Cape Ann*, which carried general freight rather than bananas, which, of course, needed refrigeration," said Captain James McNamara. "She was a rather famous ship in the late 1950s, having rescued survivors from the sinking *Andrea Doria* off Nantucket on July 26, 1956. She was, however, on a charter voyage at the time, sailing from Bremerhaven, Germany to New York."

The Alcoa Steamship Company maintained a regular service from New York down to the Eastern Caribbean and South America. Ports of call out of New York included Bermuda, St. Thomas, La Guaira, Guanta, Puerto Sucre, Trinidad, and ports in British Guiana or Surinam. Here *(right)* we see the C2-class freighter *Alcoa Roamer*, a 7,200-ton freighter with quarters for twelve passengers. "Alcoa carried lots of general freight going south and returned with the likes of bauxite and used equipment needing repairs," added Captain McNamara. The 459-foot-long *Alcoa Roamer* is berthed, in this early 1950s view, at Alcoa's pier at Cedar Street in Lower Manhattan.

Trade between New York and the east coast of South America was booming after the Second World War. The Argentine State Line handled part of this and, along with a good-sized fleet of freighters, commissioned a trio of Italian-built passenger-cargo liners. The 11,000-ton *Rio de La Plata* (*opposite, top*) at Pier 25, at Franklin Street, *Rio Jachal,* and *Rio Tunuyan,* were used for regular runs to Trinidad, Rio de Janeiro, Santos, Montevideo, and Buenos Aires. Along with six holds for freight, each ship could carry up to 116 passengers in all-first-class accommodations that included fine public rooms, a lido deck, and an outdoor pool. Fares for the 16-day voyage from New York to Buenos Aires began at $550 in the early 1950s. "Unfortunately, Argentine State Line had the messiest pier on the waterfront in those days," noted James McNamara. "The pier was actually too small and so the company was choked for space. The Rio liners had a 6-day layover, usually from Saturday morning until the following Friday afternoon. They carried most of their cargo on the northbound runs from South America. They were not necessarily very efficient, however, since they were government owned and operated and so never driven by profit or efficiency."

New York–headquartered Moore-McCormack Lines was a powerhouse in the busy trade of the 1950s and '60s to the east coast

of South America. With a large fleet of freighters along with several luxury passenger ships, there were at least two sailings from New York each week: one to Brazilian ports, the other to Brazil, Uruguay, and Argentina. Mor-Mac, as it was dubbed, also owned the American Scantic Line, which traded from New York to Scandinavian ports such as Oslo, Copenhagen, and Gdynia. Here (*opposite, bottom*) at Pier 32, Canal Street, we see one of Mor-Mac's largest freighters of the postwar era, the 7,900-ton *Mormacgulf,* which, among other cargoes, is loading railway cars for shipment bound for Argentina. "Mor-Mac had some of the best maintained heavy-lift equipment at sea in the 1950s," noted McNamara. "A specialty was to transport the likes of locomotives and railway cars."

An old veteran from the Second World War, the Liberty ship *John W. Brown* sat at Pier 42 in Greenwich Village looking much like a working ship (*above*). In fact, she never sailed, but instead served as the Food and Maritime High School, a training ship that was a part of the city's Board of Education. Her days ended in 1983, when she was towed to Baltimore and refitted as a museum ship, a testament to the great role played by the some 2,700 Liberty ships in the history of the U.S. Merchant Marine.

18

The Chelsea Piers *(opposite, top)*, stretching from West 13th to West 22nd Street along Manhattan's West Side, handled many freighters after the Second World War. Tenants included the fifty-five-ship United States Lines and another important American shipowner, the Grace Line. "The most interesting thing about this great photo is that every ship, seven in all, is American built. And they are all American owned and operated, as well," commented James McNamara. "This would not happen today. The U.S. Merchant Marine has shrunk almost beyond recognition." In this aerial view of 1951, we see (from left to right) a Grace Line freighter, the *Santa Rita*, at Pier 65; the Panama Line's *Ancon* at adjacent Pier 64; the liner *America* and the troopship *Marine Lynx* sharing Pier 61; two United States Lines freighters, the *American Planter* and *American Forwarder*; and Grace Line's *Santa Barbara* at Pier 58. To the right of the *Santa Barbara*, early construction has begun on Pier 57, the Grace Line terminal at West 15th Street that burned beyond repair in July 1947.

The Grace Line was another important shipper in the Latin American trades, but with concentrations in the Caribbean and along the west coast of South America, to Colombia, Ecuador, Peru, and Chile. Four Grace ships—one passenger and three freighters—sailed every Friday at midday and here *(opposite, bottom)* we see the C2-class *Santa Teresa* departing on her maiden voyage in 1940. "The *Santa Teresa* and her sisters were among the very first C-2 class freighters to be built," according to Captain McNamara. "With some changes in design, they led to 200 to 300 more of the same class, completed by 1945–46."

The mighty United States Lines, with some fifty-five freighters in the 1950s, offered as many as five to six ships sailing each week from New York to Dublin, London, Liverpool, Glasgow, Rotterdam, and Bremen. A subsidiary, the American Pioneer Line, traded to the Pacific, to Far Eastern ports (Yokohama, Kobe, Hong Kong, and Manila), as well as Australia and New Zealand. Arriving from a long voyage "down under," here *(left, top)*, in a 1959 view, we see the *Pioneer Isle* in the Hudson approaching her West Side berth with her forty crewmembers. Another extensive journey is complete. The piers of Hoboken are in the background, including the Holland America Line terminals with the liner *Statendam* in port.

Cargoes landing on the New York docks varied, from bundles of rags to railway locomotives. Here *(left, bottom)*, in the spring of 1964, a very special item is being lifted onto a barge by a floating crane. It is the Pieta, which has been brought from the Vatican through Naples, crossing on the liner *Cristoforo Colombo*, for a two-year loan at the 1964–65 World's Fair in Flushing Meadow. The priceless statue traveled in a special container, which rested on an aft deck aboard the Italian liner and which, it was reported, would float if the *Colombo* sank. The off-loading took place at Pier 84, with the United States Lines' freighter *American Commander* in the background.

Sending scrap metal overseas has always been a busy trade at New York harbor. In this view (*opposite, top*), dated February 13, 1958, the Danish freighter *Hedda Dan* is loading scrap by bucket lifting "goose neck" floating cranes. "The scrap was brought in by railway hopper cars and then loaded aboard ships at the Central Railroad of New Jersey piers in Jersey City," noted Captain McNamara. "Exporting scrap was a big business, especially after the Second World War." The *Exeter*, a combination passenger-cargo liner owned by American Export Lines, is outbound for the Mediterranean in the background.

Heavy-lift goods, such as steel products and machinery, often required special handling. West Germany's Hansa Line was noted for its mighty, heavy-lift cargo ships, and, in this 1975 view (*opposite, bottom*), we see the 511-foot-long *Gutenfels* taking on special cargo. The 6,800-ton ship is specially berthed in Jersey City on this occasion. "Hansa Line was a traditional heavy-lift company that was well suited to transporting heavy, as well as large cargoes," added Captain McNamara. "Here we see long cooling towers being loaded for relay to the Middle East."

Railway covered freight barges are gathered in the foreground (*left, top*), as American President Lines' *President Monroe*, a combination passenger-cargo ship with quarters for ninety-six travelers, rests at Pier 9 in Jersey City. The date is February 5, 1959. "Pier 9 was one of the port's finest piers and was leased to a high-caliber tenant, American President," reported James McNamara. "Not everyone realized, however, that the Holland Tunnel was directly underneath."

Until the early 1970s, American President Lines owned some of the largest, fastest, and finest freighters to call regularly at New York. Here (*left, middle*) we see the 9,600-ton *President Adams* inbound at New York. A fast ship with a top speed of 20 knots, she had seven holds for freight and high-standard accommodations for a dozen passengers. She was routed on American President's continuous three-month, around-the-world service, which began in the early 1960s at Jersey City and continued to Panama, California, Hawaii, Southeast Asia, India, and Pakistan, then homeward through Suez and the Mediterranean. Passenger fares for the 18-day, New York–to–San Francisco segment were posted from $300 in the mid-1950s.

United Fruit Company, with inbound ships such as the 5,000-ton *Sixaola* carrying as many as 60,000 bunches of bananas, had its own banana-handling terminal in Weehawken, New Jersey (*left, bottom*). Opened in 1950, it could handle two ships at once and had adjoining railroad connections.

The Seatrain Lines were among the most unusual shippers to use the Port of New York *(above)*. Their ships, such as the *Seatrain Georgia* and the *Seatrain Texas* (behind), were distinctive with their long, low profiles. Specially built, they had a unique purpose: carrying railway freight cars. A large, heavy-duty overhead crane was built on the company's terminal in Edgewater, New Jersey, and used until Seatrain switched to container and heavy-lift operations in the early 1970s. "Founded in 1928, Seatrain was a very special company that was actually a predecessor of unitized cargo, a pre-container carrier," noted Captain McNamara. "Malcolm McLean and his converted Sea-Land containerships actually came much later, in the mid-1950s."

In addition to United Fruit, the ships of the Standard Fruit Company were familiar sights along the lower end of the East River coming and going at Pier 14 at the foot of Wall Street in Lower Manhattan. Standard Fruit tended to use charter tonnage beginning in the 1950s, however, and here *(below)* we see the West German–flag *Polarlicht* approaching her berth following a voyage from La Ceiba and Puerto Barrois in Central America. Captain McNamara added, "German reefers were always sleek and very well maintained. They were on charter to Standard Fruit, but through Vaccaro Brothers and so the 'V' is painted on the funnels."

Pier 36 on the East River, located at the foot of Clinton Street, was the last working cargo pier in Manhattan when it closed down in the early 1990s. The only other active piers by then were the three terminals, piers 88, 90 and 92, that formed the West Side Passenger Ship Terminal. In this view *(above)* from 1970, the modern break-bulk freighter *Netuno*, operated by the Brazilian-flag Netumar Line, is being worked from both shore, as well as a barge at Pier 36. She is off-loading coffee from Rio and Santos.

Great, slender finger piers sprung out from the shoreline of Brooklyn Heights, from the bottom end of streets that were readily identifiable with the docks themselves: Remsen, Joralemon, Fulton, and Furman. While freight was the mainstay, until the late

1930s passenger ships called at this section of Brooklyn as well, namely some of the Grace Line, Munson Line, and Royal Netherlands Steamship Company. After the Second World War, some of the port's busiest and most important shipping companies, such as Moore-McCormack and Farrell Lines, leased piers in Brooklyn Heights. In this 1947 view *(below)*, the Yugoslavian freighter *Franka*, a veteran from 1918, is on the right while an unidentified, rust-covered Liberty ship, no doubt still in postwar government service, is on the left. Two of Lower Manhattan's tallest towers, the Bank of Manhattan (left) and Cities Service buildings (right), add to the poetic setting of the great port city.

Britain's Elder Dempster Lines used Pier 1 at the foot of Fulton Street in Brooklyn Heights for many years. For a port commerce documentary, a filmmaker (*above*) is recording the sailing of their exotically-named *Obuasi*, a 5,900-ton freighter, that is departing on Elder Dempster's prime service: to West African ports. She'll carry American manufactured goods to Takoradi, Lagos, Freetown, and Accra, and then return to Brooklyn (and other U.S. East Coast ports such as Boston, Philadelphia, Baltimore, and Norfolk) with bark, roots, and palm oil. This view dates from October 6, 1961.

The promenade above the busy piers of Brooklyn Heights allowed for many fascinating views, particularly of the Lower Manhattan skyline (*below*). Two of the best-known Brooklyn shipowners of the 1950s and '60s, Colombia's Grancolombiana and the Oslo-based Meyer Line, are represented. Grancolombiana's *Ciudad de Barranquilla*, inbound from Cartagena, Santa Marta, Buenaventura, Guayaquil, Callao, and her namesake port, is on the left in this 1961 photo, while the larger *Havskar* is loading for Meyer's regular North Atlantic service to Antwerp, Rotterdam, Bremen, and Hamburg.

Japan's NYK Line (Nippon Yusen Kaisha), was revived after the Second World War and, by the early 1950s, resumed their long-distance service between New York, Yokohama, and Kobe via the Panama Canal. Trade, size, and speed of the NYK ships soon increased. In a scene dated January 16, 1962, at Pier 7 in Brooklyn Heights *(above)*, we see the 9,500-ton *Suruga Maru* in the foreground and her twin sister, the *Sagami Maru*, just behind. They would be off-loading cargoes such as silks and foodstuffs, and then departing with cargo such as American-made machinery and manufactured goods. "By the 1960s, the Japanese had an increasingly larger presence in New York harbor. Their ships seemed to be everywhere," noted Captain McNamara. Across Pier 7, but on a far different route from the western Mediterranean to New York, are Costa Line's *Francesco "C"* and the Swedish-flag Norton Line freighter (on charter from the Salen Line). They would have been assigned to the east coast of South America run, carrying coffee

from Rio, Santos, Bahia, and Fortaleza. The Staten Island ferry terminal, located at Whitehall in Lower Manhattan, can be seen across the mouth of the East River.

The cargo ships of Denmark's Maersk Line were very distinctive in New York harbor because of their blue hulls. Ship's names were also vividly painted along the sides. Maersk, which had grown by 2004 to be the largest container-cargo operator in the world, had great interests in the 1950s and '60s in the New York–Asian Far East trades. In this 1959 view *(below)*, it is something of a special occasion—the 6,400-ton *Laust Maersk* has just arrived on her maiden voyage to the port, and is berthed at Brooklyn's Pier 11 across from her sister ship, the *Marit Maersk*, and an older fleetmate, the *Jeppesen Maersk*, can be seen on the left. Today, Maersk is the largest container-cargo company in the world. "Maersk is totally subsidized by the Danish government," added Captain McNamara, "and so there are no losses, no true competition."

Brooklyn's Atlantic Basin, located off Atlantic Avenue in the Red Hook section, was one of the port's most modern and active terminals by the 1960s. Here *(right, top)* we see American automobiles being loaded aboard Prudential Lines' *Newberry Victory*, which will sail for the Mediterranean to Genoa, Piraeus, and Istanbul. Just beyond, off-loading freight from the likes of Singapore, Manila, Hong Kong, and Kobe is Maersk Line's *Jeppesen Maersk*. "American cars were big exports through the 1960s," added Captain McNamara. "They were known throughout the world and were very much in demand."

Floating grain elevators, two of which are seen here *(right, bottom)*, were among the port's more eccentric craft. They were owned by the International Elevating Company and based at piers at Essex Street in Jersey City. All of them were retired, however, by 1958. In this busy scene, near Brooklyn's Erie Basin, we see grain being transferred from an otherwise mothballed, Fort-class freighter of World War II vintage (left), and transferred to another wartime ship, the still active Greek-flag *Hellenic Star*. The grain is destined for the Piraeus in Greece and other Eastern Mediterranean ports. A U.S. Navy landing ship, undergoing dockside repairs, is on the upper right.

One of Brooklyn's longest docks, the Columbia Street Pier *(opposite, top)*, could handle four large freighters at one time. Along with some railroad barges, a railway carfloat, and a floating crane, are the Norwegian-flag Fern Line freighter, the *Ferngulf* (left) and the *New York Maru* (right) of Japan's Kawasaki Shipping Company, commonly known as the K Line. A Liberty ship owned by Bethlehem Steel's Calmar Steamship Company is moored at the Port Authority Grain Elevator, which was built in 1921, and with the Ira S. Bushey Shipyard, which serviced smaller ships and harborcraft (far right). In the distance are two of what were, in the 1960s, Brooklyn's tallest buildings: the 37-story tower known as 16 Court Street (left) and the 42-story Williamsburg Savings Bank (right).

To meet their expanding needs and support a brand-new fleet of modern freighters beginning in the early 1960s, Moore-McCormack Lines moved to a specially built terminal located at the foot of 23rd Street in Brooklyn. Here *(opposite, bottom)* we see it on something of a banner day in 1964: no less than six Mor-Mac freighters are berthed together. To the left are two cargo ships belonging to the Caribbean-routed Bull Line and, at the far left, one from the Hamburg American Line. In the lower right is a small section of Bethlehem Steel's shipyard, located at the bottom end of 27th Street and soon to be closed.

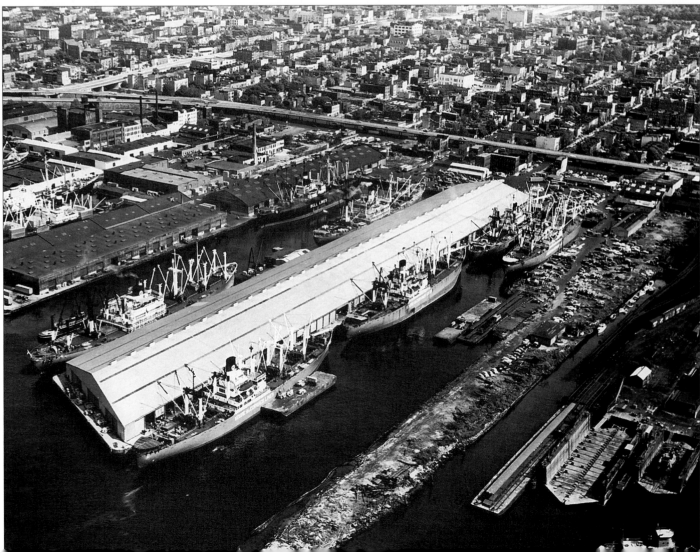

Norwegian-flag Hoegh Lines used one of Brooklyn's best-known shipping facilities, the 1905-built Bush Terminal. With eight long piers, it stretched for ten Brooklyn blocks, covering 150 acres of land, as well as 900,000 square feet of adjoining warehouse space. It even had its own railroad that included nine diesel locomotives, one tugboat, and nine railroad carfloats. In this 1961 view *(above)*, we see the brand-new, 9,800-ton *Hoegh Dyke* arriving in the Upper Bay for the first time. Along with a sizeable cargo capacity and comfortable quarters for forty-five crew and twelve passengers, the 17-knot ship will be assigned to the New York–Middle East run. She would be routed on itineraries to Alexandria, Bombay, Karachi, Calcutta, and Madras. "Hoegh was one of the best run freighter companies in New York in the 1960s," noted Captain McNamara. "Their ships were always immaculate."

Another maiden voyage: the 536-foot-long *Karakorum*, a 10,900-tonner that belongs to the Dutch-flag Nederland Line *(below)*. Dressed in flags and with a Moran tug snuggled alongside for assistance, she and her sisters were, in the early '60s, noted as being among the mightiest cargo liners to call regularly at the port. Useful for her Middle and Far Eastern voyages, which often included U.S.-manufactured steel products, the heavy-lift booms attached to the third mast were capable on their own of handling loads of up to 175 tons.

The great swing over to the more expansive and more modern docks of New Jersey, first at Port Newark and later at Port Elizabeth, began in earnest in the 1950s. Within a decade, three-quarters of

the port's ship operators had relocated, leaving Manhattan, Hoboken, and Brooklyn docks all but deserted. For the Jersey facilities, gone were the one- and two-story finger piers, their limited storage capabilities, and crowded street-side access. Furthermore, the new, far more efficient age of container shipping required vast marshaling spaces, as well as the subsequent erection of large, bird-like cranes. Among the first major shipping agents to relocate to Port Newark was Norton, Lilly & Company, which looked after the New York operations of such noted British shipowners as the Ellerman Lines, Federal Steam Navigation Company, and New Zealand Shipping Company. One of Ellerman's newest and largest freighters, the *City of Sydney*, is seen here *(opposite, top)*, in July 1962, arriving at Port Newark. The arch of the New Jersey Turnpike Bridge is to the left. The 10,200-ton *City of Sydney* is carrying, among other goods, a 40-foot-long sloop on her foredeck. She is arriving from Liverpool and other British ports, then will load American manufactured goods for a long voyage via Panama to Sydney, Melbourne, and other Australian ports and finally, after being reloaded with a valuable cargo of meat and wool, will sail homeward to the UK via the Suez.

Even the legendary French Line, the Compagnie Generale Transatlantique, moved their cargo operations to New Jersey. In this 1962 view *(opposite, bottom)*, the 488-foot-long cargo liner *Le Moyne D'Ibreville* is taking on steel products for a voyage to Le Havre.

Initially, most freighter companies began a combination of traditional break-bulk shipping, with only a few small containers stowed on deck. Here (*opposite, top*) we see a Greek freighter, a ship formerly belonging to Norway's Wilhelmsen Lines, docked at Port Elizabeth in 1975 and being "worked" with both cargo methods.

Apart from often waiting at anchor in the Narrows for berths, oil tankers tended to use berths in New Jersey at docks in areas such as Bayonne, Sewaren, Carteret, Elizabeth, and Bayway. Tankers grew considerably in size following the Second World War and the increasing demand for oil fuels. In this view in the Lower Bay (*opposite, bottom*), the brand-new *Esso New York* arrives for the first time. An 18,000-ton vessel of 628 feet, she and her ten sisters were considered "supertankers" when built in the late 1940s. Each ship had a capacity for 230,000 barrels of oil, or more than 9,600,000 gallons in all.

Here (*above*) we see one of the largest U.S.-flag tankers of the 1960s, the 58,000-ton *National Defender*, being assisted by a Moran tug in the Kill van Kull.

CHAPTER THREE
Luxury Liner Row: The Great Passenger Ships

"Part of the great fun of going to Europe began with the trip to the West Side in Manhattan to catch the boat," remembered Kitty Carlisle Hart: actress, television personality, and widow of playwright Moss Hart. "It was all very exciting, seeing the big liners for the first time, going aboard, settling into your stateroom, and then having one of those bon voyage parties. Packing for the trip was a nightmare, however. We had those big, bulky wardrobe trunks with the bottom shelf just for shoes. They were yellow-brown, had brass locks, but always troublesome. To unlock them, you often would have a set of bloodied knuckles. And, of course, we had hat boxes, as well."

Jane Bouche Strong remembered her many departures on the French Line. "By the time you had embarked on your second Transat [for Compagnie Generale Transatlantique] voyage, you were well on your way to becoming a *passager fidèle*, one of the faithful, and were treated accordingly. Your name, preferences, and even your birthday were remembered. For such an occasion, the chief purser [onboard a crossing on the *Liberte*] invited us to lunch in a small private dining room. The champagne flowed. Afterward, he escorted us to his sitting room for coffee and Calvados. On a center table was a champagne bucket filled with flowers, but of a curious scent; they had been carved out of carrots, leeks, and turnips!"

Many other New Yorkers have vivid recollections of those great West Side piers and the grand ships that used them. Keen ship enthusiast Richard Morse decided to spend his fourteenth birthday with the liners and remembered, "Saturday, January 21, 1939, was a cold, cloudy, blustery winter day, with occasional snow flurries just to spice things up. The grayness of the harbor was relieved only by the colorful smokestacks of Atlantic liners docked at their Hudson River piers. It looked like this: At 57th Street, we could see the single yellow funnel of the *Drottningholm*, with her characteristic three yellow crowns on a blue disc; sharing her pier was the *Monarch of Bermuda*, proudly displaying her red and black Furness colors. A few blocks south, at 52nd Street, the Italian Line's *Vulcania*, sporting a single short motorship funnel (white, with a green band and red top), was preparing to depart for the Mediterranean at noon. Next to her, on the north side of Pier 90, was the magnificent *Aquitania*, that beloved old Cunarder, proudly flaunting her four orange and black stacks and smoking away, preparatory to an eleven o'clock sailing for the Channel ports. Her neighbor, at the French Line pier, was my first love among ocean liners, the *Ile de France*, making ready for an 11:30 departure, also for England and France. Continuing south, we would encounter the *Columbus* of North German Lloyd, with a 5:00 P.M. sailing on a 13-day cruise to the Caribbean. Finally, at West 44th Street was the *New York*, the Hamburg America Line flagship unloading from a previous day's arrival from Europe. Her light buff-colored stacks with red, white, and black tops contrasted sharply with the plain mustard-colored funnels of the *Columbus*.

Of course, the *Ile de France* showed her three deep red with black top funnels to complete the palette."

Morse continued, "Thus it was when I celebrated my fourteenth birthday, assisted by my brother. A walk of three long blocks from the 9th Avenue Elevated took us to Luxury Liner Row. There we made a beeline for that temple of seagoing Art Deco, the *Ile de France*. There she was, just begging to be explored.

"We paid a dime apiece and went up 'The Longest Gangplank in the World,' as the French Line called it. The two of us just reveled in the magnificence of the *Ile*'s decor. We visited the main lounge, first-class dining room, the chapel, and looked at a few first-class staterooms. What a way to go! Here was opulence almost unknown to us teenagers, though to tell the truth, we had been aboard several big luxury liners to see relatives off. It still took some getting used to. We wandered all over, mostly in first class, and ended up on the port side promenade deck, facing the neighboring Cunard–White Star pier. We suddenly heard much triple-chime-type hooting, and looking up, saw four huge Cunard funnels moving riverward: the *Aquitania* was sailing on schedule. It was an unforgettable sight, seeing those big black and orange stacks backing out in the midst of a dreary winter snow flurry. It was time to go, the *Ile de France* was sailing in half an hour, and we had to visit my aunt in the hospital."

After the Second World War, in the 1950s and '60s, Harold Oshzy made many business trips to and from Europe—all of them by sea. He crossed twenty-two times, for example, on the world's fastest liner, the brilliant *United States* and remembered her well. "She was a magnificent ship. Pure engineering brilliance! She had the most modern cargo capabilities at the time as well. You could travel with your car with such ease. Within twenty minutes after arrival at New York or Southampton, you could be on your way. She was, however, not the best-run ship on the North Atlantic. The service was all-American, not the grand style of, say, Cunard or the French. The crew was all union—like Lindy's waiters. There wasn't any fussing."

Oshzy took many other liners in and out of New York and remembered many of them "The *Queen Mary* was the greatest roller at sea. But she had great style. She was like the *Normandie*—one of the grand luxury liners from before the war, from the 1930s. The *Queen Elizabeth* never quite had the same feel, the same sense of grandeur. The *Ile de France* was one of my favorites. It seemed that there were more chefs onboard than passengers. Typically, the *Nieuw Amsterdam* was immaculate, truly the cleanest ship on the Atlantic. There was also great glamour to sailing in those days. Many passengers in first class crossed with their own servants and traveled with lots of those big trunks. I remember the Duke and Duchess of Windsor on the *United States*, Merle Oberon on the *Queen Mary*, and Ginger Rogers on the *Ile de France*."

From about 1905 to the mid-1930s, the hub of great ocean liner activity at New York was centered around the Chelsea Piers, a series of eight, long finger piers jutting out into the Hudson, from West 13th to West 22nd street. The docks were, in fact, built especially for a new, much larger generation of ocean liners, beginning in 1907 with the 32,000-ton, 790-foot-long *Mauretania* and her near-sister *Lusitania*. Projected superships such as the 46,000-ton, 880-foot-long sisters *Olympic* and *Titanic* in 1911–12 and the 48,000-ton, 901-foot-long *Aquitania* in 1913 could also dock there. Projections actually fell short and extensions had to be erected on piers 54 and 61 to handle this new breed of "Atlantic behemoths," as they were called. In this panoramic view (*above*), from 1935, the Chelsea Piers are in their twilight as the greatest ocean liner berths. New, larger piers are already in the works, but farther along the Hudson, between West 48th and West 52nd streets. From top left to far right, we can see the *Eastern Prince* of the Prince Line and

the *Cristobal* of the Panama Steamship Company. At the Chelsea Piers themselves: the *Washington*, United States Lines; *Georgic* and then the much larger *Majestic*, both Cunard–White Star; the laid up, rusting *Leviathan* of the United States Lines; the Red Star Line's *Pennland*; the *Paris* of the French Line; and finally Grace Line's *Santa Lucia*.

An American seamen's strike saw fourteen U.S.-flag passenger ships tied-up in New York for more than a week in September 1939. Nine of them are shown here (*below*), moored along the Chelsea Piers (from left to right): *Santa Paula*, Grace Line, at Pier 57; the *American Merchant*, *American Traveler*, *President Harding*, and the *Washington*, all United States Lines, at piers 58 and 59; the *Uruguay*, American Republics Line, at Pier 60; the *Acadia*, Eastern Steamship Lines and the *Shawnee*, Clyde Mallory Lines (outer end), sharing one side of Pier 61; and finally the *St. John*, also Eastern Steamship Lines, at Pier 62.

"You could go aboard and explore these great liners at will. It was like entering fantasyland, seeing those magnificent lounges, the lavish staterooms, and all those well-dressed, very excited, European-bound passengers," recalled the late John Gillespie, who lived nearby in a tenement on West 21st Street and Tenth Avenue. "It was a wonderful way to spend, say, a Saturday morning or, at night, to see off a midnight sailing. It was a great way also to have a date: ten cents each to board the ship, walk about and even have a dance or two in the ballroom. A glass of beer was a nickel. Afterward, we would watch from the outer end of the pier as the glowing liner departed. They made magical sights!" In this view (*opposite, top*) from 1935, we see the *Ile de France* making a midday departure for England and France from Pier 57.

Ocean liners provided idyllic escapes in those otherwise lean, troubled years of the Great Depression. For secretaries, school-teachers, and civil servants, all of which had secure jobs, there was a 4-day-long weekend cruise up to Halifax, Nova Scotia, and back for $45, or 5 days to Bermuda for $55. Here (*opposite, bottom*) we see Cunard–White Star's *Georgic* departing from Pier 61, in 1939, on a short Fourth of July weekend cruise up to Halifax and back.

Perhaps the most exciting arrivals of the mid-1930s were the first appearances of the world's largest, fastest, and most luxurious liners yet built, France's *Normandie* in June 1935 and then, almost exactly a year later, Britain's *Queen Mary*, in May 1936. Dozens of boats, tugs, fireboats, yachts, and ferries came out to welcome the "new royalty" of Atlantic liners. Horns and whistles seemed to sound without end, while thousands lined the waterfront on both sides. In this smoke-filled view (*above*), we see the brilliant *Normandie* as she slowly and graciously makes her way along the Hudson off West 10th Street.

Well before they boarded the new French flagship, onlookers were awed by the size of *Normandie*'s bow (*left*), which towered above the bottom end of West 48th Street.

The new Luxury Liner Row piers had their greatest day yet when five Atlantic liners were berthed together at piers 86, 88, and 90 in March 1937 *(above)*. To help celebrate, planes dropped tons of confetti that drifted with the wind, as the *Normandie* became the first of them to depart for Europe. The four stern sections to the right belong to (from top to bottom): the *Berengaria* and *Georgic*, Cunard–White Star; the *Rex*, Italian Line; and the *Europa*, North German Lloyd.

French Line's *Ile de France* was one of the most beloved and most popular of all liners that called at the West Side. She introduced Art-Deco designs to ocean liner decoration and style when she was first commissioned in 1927, and was noted as having the finest kitchens on the Atlantic run, the cheeriest mood, and even the longest bars. She was a favorite to millions, making almost continuous runs between New York, England, and France. In this poetic view *(below)*, she is arriving at Pier 88 on a misty morning in 1938. Taxicabs are lined up, awaiting passengers and their luggage.

Even the slightest accident among the great liners, most of them known to millions, made news. On November 11, 1937, for example *(above)*, Italy's *Rex* (right) grazed the stern of Cunard Line's *Aquitania* (left) while docking between Piers 90 and 92. Although there was no damage, the news was important enough to make all the following day's newspapers.

Tense and changing times! On August 28, 1939, American authorities decided not to allow the Nazi-German flagship *Bremen* to sail with passengers on what was to be an ordinary sailing to Cherbourg, Southampton, and finally her home port of Bremerhaven. Officials stressed that the 51,000-ton liner required further inspection for possible war materials going abroad from an otherwise cautious, very neutral American port. The 938-foot-long ship, seen here *(below)* having a routine lifeboat drill along the

south side of Pier 86, at the foot of West 46th Street, was, however, finally allowed to sail, but without passengers, on the 29th. Crewmembers lined the outer decks on the evening departure, all of them giving the raised-arm Nazi salute to the city. The Nazis invaded Poland three days later, on September 1, and the war in Europe officially started on September 3. For safety, the *Bremen* traveled on a far northern route, passing through Arctic waters, reaching Murmansk, and then clinging to the Norwegian coastline for her final return to home waters. Repainted in gray while at sea, she finally reached her Bremerhaven berth that December. But sadly, the great liner was never to sail again. Laid up during the early years of the war, she was sabotaged by an anti-Nazi youth in March 1941 and set afire. Her subsequent remains had to be scrapped.

On September 1, 1939, the *Queen Mary*, coming westbound from Southampton and Cherbourg with 2,139 nervous passengers and 1,112 crewmembers aboard, reached the safety of New York. Rumors were rife that a secret agreement had been reached between Washington, London, and Berlin in which if the *Bremen* was allowed to return to Germany, the *Queen Mary* would be left unharmed by Nazi U-boats on her voyage to America. Here *(above)* we see the Italian Line's *Roma*, continuing in commercial transatlantic service to Mussolini's still-neutral Italy, at Pier 92; then the just-arrived *Queen Mary* at Cunard's Pier 90; and finally the *Normandie*, already laid up at Pier 88.

The post–World War II era brought a boon to Atlantic liner travel, and the West Side was again, in the 1950s in particular, bustling and busy. There were many occasions when the great liners were in port together and these exciting scenes often appeared in the following day's newspapers. Here *(below)*, in a February 1956 view, we have no less than nine liners in port at the same time. From top to bottom are the *Empress of Scotland*, Canadian Pacific Steamships; the *Franconia*, *Mauretania*, *Queen Mary*, and *Caronia*, all Cunard; French Line's *Ile de France*; the *America* of United States Lines; *Andrea Doria*, Italian Line; and *Constitution*, American Export Lines.

Among the best-known ships along the West Side were Cunard's two mighty "Queens," the immensely popular and beloved *Queen Mary* and her consort the slightly larger *Queen Elizabeth*. The *Queen Mary*, seen here *(top, left)* in a 1951 photo when thick fog has delayed her departure from Pier 90, was widely known. She was the flagship of the British Merchant Fleet, as well as of the Cunard Line itself. She also broke the Atlantic speed record and served as a valiant troopship in World War II. In commercial transatlantic service, she and the *Elizabeth* sailed almost every Wednesday on 5-day passages to Cherbourg and Southampton. Fares in the early '50s, for example, began at $370 in first class, $250 in cabin class, and $175 in tourist class. The two ships were often booked to capacity a year in advance, especially in peak summer.

A great Manhattan tradition was to see off the great liners from their West Side berths. Even for their mid-week, midday sailings, as many as 5,000 family members, friends, and general well-wishers were there as the 2,000 passengers departed onboard the likes of the *Queen Elizabeth*, seen here *(below)* in a 1947 view. The 83,673-ton *Elizabeth* was the largest liner afloat from 1940 until 1996 and, along with the *Queen Mary*, were part of the noblest maritime royalty along Luxury Liner Row.

The Cunard "Queens" were particulary palatial, grand, and impeccably maintained ships in their heyday. They were also immensely popular and profitable. In first class especially, travelers lived in a world of polished woods, glistening chandeliers, working fireplaces, and carpets so thick that your shoes almost disappeared from view. The perfectly uniformed staff had often been with the Cunard Company for decades, and sometimes followed earlier relatives in service and considered it a prized position to serve aboard the ships, especially one of the two "Queens." Here *(top, right)* we see the magnificent first-class smoking room aboard the 2,223-passenger *Queen Elizabeth*.

Cunard was only liner company in the 1950s to occupy two West Side piers. They had the largest liner fleet on the Atlantic and, in 1958, it numbered no less than twelve passenger ships in all. There was also two dozen or so freighters in Cunard service. In this busy summer's day *(above)*, we see four Cunarders: the *Georgic* (top) is still docked on the south side of Pier 90, from which the *Queen Mary* is just departing from the north berth. At Pier 92, the *Mauretania* (middle) is preparing to sail later the same day while the combination passenger-cargo ship *Media*, being worked by cargo and railway barges, is at the bottom.

In the '50s, there were over one hundred marine reporters in and around New York harbor, and one of their prime tasks was to interview and photograph celebrities aboard the great liners *(below)*. Usually, these sessions took place on the inbound voyages, with the reporters climbing aboard from a launch or tug in the Lower Bay and then often finishing the interviews and photo sessions by the time the liners reached the West Side piers. The following day's newspapers often carried photos and sometimes accompanying articles on royalty, politicians, authors, but most of all, Hollywood and Broadway stars. The obligatory "cheesecake" photos were, not surprisingly, the most popular.

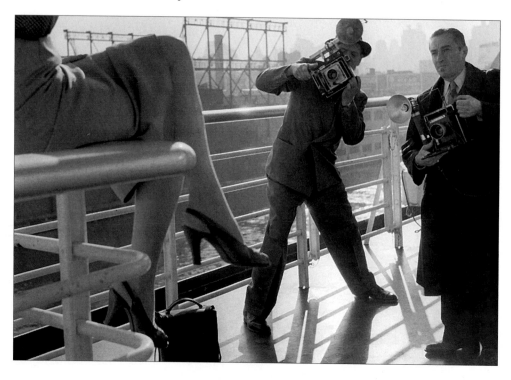

Wrapped in mink, actress Marie McDonald (*above, left*), is bundled up against the chilly New York morning of December 20, 1955, as she arrives aboard the *Ile de France*.

Hollywood entertainers Tony Martin and Cyd Charisse (*above, right*), strike up a pose sure to delight reporters and photographers as they headed for a European vacation aboard the *United States* in 1958.

Italian film queen Anna Magnani (*middle*), gives a cheerful wave as she prepares to set sail on the *Andrea Doria* in 1955.

By far the most photographed of all Atlantic passengers in the 1950s and '60s were the Duke and Duchess of Windsor. They crossed twice each year, in winter and in June, between their home in Paris and the social circuit of New York, Long Island, and West Palm Beach. It was a considerable undertaking just for the 5-day sea voyage: ninety-eight pieces of luggage including thirty large trunks, their own linens and china, personal objects d'art for their three-room interconnecting suite, and as many as five silver, gold-coin enhanced serving bowls for their beloved pets. They are seen here (*right*), with one of their five dogs, as they arrive in New York in March 1966 from Le Havre aboard the *United States*.

The *Mauretania*, a ship completed in 1939 and the second to bear that legendary name, was a very popular Cunarder. Many preferred her, for example, because she was not quite as large, or as hotel-like, as the *Queen Mary* and *Queen Elizabeth*, and because, being somewhat slower, she had an added day of sea travel on her crossings between New York, Cobh, Le Havre, and Southampton. She is seen here (*above*), just after her postwar return to service in April 1947, outbound in the Hudson. The busy Chelsea Docks are in the background and, among many freighters, the liner *America*—the flagship of the entire U.S. Merchant Marine—is at berth, pausing between her own North Atlantic schedule of sailings.

Cunard's green-colored *Caronia*, which first arrived in New York in January 1949, was said by many to be the "most luxurious ocean liner afloat." Indeed, she might have been. It was said only Cunard's finest, handpicked staff served aboard her. Dubbed "the millionaires' yacht," she could carry up to 932 passengers, but was usually limited to 600. She often carried as few as 300 passengers, all looked after by 600 staff members. While she occasionally made an ordinary Atlantic crossing, her mainstay was long, luxurious, expensive cruises: one hundred or so days around the world each winter, six weeks to the Mediterranean in spring, six weeks to Scandinavia and Northern Europe in summer, and then eight weeks back to the Mediterranean in fall. It was a luxurious pattern comfortable to many, in fact some passengers "lived aboard" for years at a time and one lady could boast of fourteen years of continuous *Caronia* cruising. The 34,000-ton liner is seen here (*below*), preparing for a mostly warm-weather trip around the world, but in an ice-filled Hudson River on a night in January 1955. French Line's *Liberte* is to the left at Pier 88.

American passenger ships were noted especially for their pristine upkeep and modern interior decor. Built in 1940 and then used during the Second World War as the troopship USS *West Point*, the 33,500-ton *America* was considered the finest, fastest, and best decorated ship in the U.S. Merchant Marine in the late '40s. She is seen here *(above)* departing from her Chelsea berth at Pier 61, at West 21st Street with the Bethlehem Steel Shipyard in Hoboken in the background. Meseck tugs are looking after the 723-foot-long liner.

Excitement fills the air! European-bound passengers board the *America* in this 1949 view *(below)*.

When the American Export Lines took delivery of their brand-new ocean liner sisters *Independence* and *Constitution*, it was a high-point in the history of not only the U.S. Merchant Marine, but in overall passenger ship history. The twin 29,500-tonners were fast, big, modern, and revolutionary: they were the first fully air-conditioned luxury liners built. Their amenities were statements in themselves on the innovative standards of American design and development: individual climatic control in every passenger state-room, other cabins easily convertible from bedrooms to daytime sit-ting rooms, lighted outdoor pools, and even Coca-Cola bars. The two sisters were a huge success, carrying up to 1,000 passengers each in three classes on three-week roundtrips between New York, Algeciras (in Spain), Naples, Genoa, Cannes, and back to Algeciras before returning to New York. In this view *(opposite, top left)*, on the cold morning of January 22, 1951, the 683-foot-long *Independence* arrives off American Export's Pier 84 for the first time. She had been built by Bethlehem Steel at their Quincy, Massachusetts plant and has come down on a gala introductory mini-cruise from Boston.

The superliner *United States* seemed to grab almost all the head-lines following her triumphant July 1952 maiden voyage when she captured the prized Blue Riband. With a record-breaking speed of 3 days, 10 hours, and 40 minutes between New York's Ambrose Light and Bishop's Rock in Cornwall, England, the $72 million maritime masterpiece of Yankee design and engineering shaved over 10 hours off the *Queen Mary*'s existing record. Although a tightly kept military secret at the time, the 53,000-ton, 990-foot-long *United States* had an extraordinary 240,000 horsepower. She was also said to be the safest ship afloat, with the only wood aboard being the Steinway piano and the butcher's blocks. She was also strong, very modern, and spotlessly maintained. She also had two of the biggest funnels ever to go to sea, as exemplified in this view *(oppo-site, top right)*. She was a wondrous ship in every way and everyone, so it seemed, wanted to sail in her, or at least visit her. In the 1950s, she was the most popular single liner on the North Atlantic.

Ocean liner heroics! The *Ile de France* unexpectedly returned to Pier 88 on July 27, 1956, with 758 survivors from the disastrous *Andrea Doria–Stockholm* collision off Nantucket on the foggy night of the 25th. Mortally pierced by the Swedish liner's bow, the Italian took on great amounts of seawater, began to continually list, and then sank the following morning. Among the rescue ships, all which returned to New York, the Le Havre–bound *Ile de France* was the most gallant, transporting the greatest number of passen-gers and crew *(opposite, bottom left)*. With her schedule dis-rupted, she immediately sailed again for Europe.

The German superliner *Europa*, well known to New Yorkers in her prewar career, sat out the Second World War neglected, rust-ing at her homeport of Bremerhaven. The Nazi high command chose not to use her, and the 936-foot liner was seized by invading American forces in May 1945. After a stint as the transport USS *Europa*, she was given to the French as reparations and, after a lengthy refit, was resurrected for transatlantic service in August 1950 as the *Liberte*. For the next eleven years, until her final sailing in November 1961, she was one of the port's most popular and noted liners. "No company served more caviar, or had better menus in any class, than the French Line," remembered Ruth Gordon. "They were the epitome of Atlantic ocean liners." The 51,000-ton *Liberte* is seen here *(opposite, bottom right)* in a poetic view through a cargo-loading door on Pier 88.

One of the port's most embarrassing moments involved the French. In July 1952, on her flag-bedecked maiden voyage, the 20,500-ton *Flandre*, in fact the first newly built French-Atlantic liner since the 1930s, had a massive mechanical breakdown. When she reached the Lower Bay, she could not even raise her anchor, or sound her whistle. Consequently, Moran tugs had to tow the 600-foot ship into port as other ships signaled greetings and welcomes with their whistles. The 22-knot ship is seen here *(above)* being berthed by Moran tugs on the north side of Pier 88. United States Lines' *America* is behind.

The *France*, seen here *(opposite, top)* passing Lower Manhattan, was commissioned in February 1962 and was the last of the great French liners to sail the Atlantic. Although she had far more modern, somewhat less grand, and often rather basic decorative styles, she continued the great French traditions of flawless cooking, exemplary service, and a seagoing style surpassed by no other. In first class, for example, there were said to be "buckets" of Beluga caviar that were served with soupspoons and the greatest wine cellar on the ocean. She was also the last liner to have daily menus for pets. Her passengers were said to be the best dressed on the Atlantic—film stars in particular favored her—and that the purser's department still maintained ledgers of past passengers and their preferences. Unfortunately, the $80 million ship was built too late, she was losing money by the late '60s and had to be subsidized by the French Government (up to $14 million a year in the end). She was retired in September 1974 after only twelve years on the Le Havre–New York run.

As part of post–World War II penalties, West Germany was not permitted to own large liners for ten years, until 1955, or build any for ten more. It was therefore a momentous day in July 1959 when two West German liners, the *Berlin* (left) and the *Bremen* (right), passed one another off the Battery *(opposite, bottom)*. It was the first time, in fact, that two German liners were together in New York since that fateful summer of 1939. The stripped, much reduced North German Lloyd, which had owned two of the largest and fastest liners afloat, the *Bremen* and the *Europa* in the 1930s, had to make do with secondhand passenger ships. The 19,100-ton, 1925-built *Gripsholm*, which hoisted the West German colors in January 1955 and became the *Berlin* was the first, followed four years later by the 32,000-ton *Bremen*, which had been extensively rebuilt and modernized after having been the French *Pasteur*, originally built in 1939.

Another German liner sailed along the Hudson for the first time on July 25, 1962. She was officially called *Bremen IV, Junior.* It is seen here *(above)* off the Battery with United Fruit's *Yaque* in the background. This 39-foot-long working-scale model of the original 51,000-ton *Bremen* of 1929 had two men inside the 10-ton recreation, which had been brought from Germany aboard a freighter, the *Neckarstein*. The model went on tour in the United States before returning to Germany.

A liner with lots of troubles at New York was Poland's *Batory.* Revived after Second World War service as an Allied trooper, she resumed her sailings from Gdynia and Copenhagen to great popularity. However, beginning in May 1949, in the age of the Cold War, the ship's image became increasingly tarnished. American dockers, in particular, resented her supposed Polish-Soviet ownership. Later, an accused Communist spy was said to have escaped aboard the 14,200-ton ship from New York, with the captain's approval no less. The newspaper headlines were damaging. In the end, New York stevedores and even shipyard workers refused to handle the ship. In January 1951, her Atlantic schedules were abruptly cancelled and the 18-knot vessel was refitted for a far different service: Northern Europe to India and Pakistan. In this view *(below)*, she is seen arriving off Pier 88.

A most unusual and distinctive visitor to Luxury Liner Row was the sumptuous yacht *Christina* (**opposite, top**), owned by Greek tycoon Aristotle Onassis. She was moored at Cunard's Pier 92 in April 1961, having crossed the mid-Atlantic with Onassis and his special guests Sir Winston and Lady Churchill onboard. The 300-foot-long vessel was said to be the most luxurious yacht then afloat. The swimming pool floor, for example, was a mosaic of acrobats and bulls done in lazuli, the water could be either heated or chilled and the bottom could be raised by night to create a dance floor surrounded by lighted jets of spraying water. A nearby bar had stools made of whale bones and a twin-engine Piaggio amphibious aircraft was cradled in the stern and used to carry guests, as well as fetch mail and daily newspapers. The 1,850-ton vessel had been extravagantly rebuilt in the mid-1950s at a Hamburg shipyard where Onassis was also building some of the largest oil tankers of the day. The *Christina* had been a Canadian frigate, built in 1943 and later bought by Onassis at auction. He had her gutted and remade as his "floating palace."

Mishaps were almost always recorded. Here (**opposite, middle**), Swedish American Line's *Gripsholm* arrives at Pier 97 with damage to her port bow section after a slight collision with a Norwegian freighter.

Weather often wreaked havoc with schedules, especially those rigidly fixed for passenger liners. On her last westbound sailing from Gothenburg and Copenhagen to New York in February 1948, Swedish American Line's *Drottningholm* encountered the "worst weather" of her entire 43-year career. Her master, Captain John Nordlander said, "The waves were so high and so fierce that fourteen-inch-wide panes of glass along the promenade deck were broken." Passengers shown here (**opposite, bottom**) managed a cheery greeting through the ice-encased windows as the ship finally docked at Pier 97 two days late.

With her bow gone, and the remains badly crushed, the 12,000-ton *Stockholm* (**above**), returned to Pier 97 on July 27, 1956 following her tragic collision with the pride of the Italian fleet, the *Andrea Doria*. Fifty-two people perished, and to many the 525-foot-long Swede was the villain. She was soon moved to a Brooklyn shipyard to begin over four months of repairs. In this scene above the West Side Highway at 57th Street, the *Ocean Monarch* and *Queen of Bermuda* of the Furness-Bermuda Lines are together at Pier 95 while Cunard's *Mauretania* is in mid-river, about to begin another Atlantic voyage.

The 29,000-ton *Andrea Doria* was dubbed Italy's "renaissance ship" when she first arrived in New York harbor in January 1953. She is seen here *(opposite, top)* in the Lower Bay. She signaled the postwar rebirth of the Italian Merchant Marine, and in particular their celebrated liner fleet, following the devastation of Mussolini's Italy. The 700-foot-long *Doria* was among the port's most modern, best fed and served, and reportedly safest ocean liners. She ran as part of Italian Line's express service: New York to Gibraltar in 6 days, to Naples in 8 days, and to Genoa and Cannes in 9 days. Unfortunately, the 1,248-passenger *Doria*'s days were numbered. Due at Pier 84 on July 26, 1956, she was rammed in thick fog off Nantucket Island the night before by the Swedish American liner *Stockholm*. Mortally struck below the starboard bridge, the *Doria* quickly began to flood and then, abandoned by passengers and crew, rolled and sank the next morning. The staff at the Italian Line's Lower Manhattan offices was stunned.

The *Andrea Doria*'s twin sister, the *Cristoforo Colombo*, first arrived in New York in the summer of 1954. She became the national flagship following the *Doria*'s loss in 1956 until surpassed in size, speed, and luxury by the new *Leonardo da Vinci* in June 1960. Following the sinking of the *Andrea Doria*, Italian Line and other passenger lines seemed more interested in reassuring the public, particularly potential passengers, of their emphasis on safety and rescue. Here *(opposite, bottom)*, on March 25, 1960, on the north side of Pier 84, a complete lifeboat drill is underway aboard the *Colombo*.

Faced with the unbeatable competition of the airlines, as well as increasing labor problems by the highly unionized Italian crew, the Italian Line, like so many others, began to wind down their money-losing New York services in the late 1960s and early '70s. Luxurious new ships such as the 45,000-ton sisters *Michelangelo* and *Raffaello* never earned a profit and so sailed for a mere ten years before being retired in 1975. The *Leonardo da Vinci*, seen here *(right, top)* on the left in this scene from January 1969 as the *Michelangelo* is docking, made the last New York–Italy sailing for the Italian Line in the spring of 1976.

The week or so before Christmas often created great gatherings of ocean liners along the West Side. Almost all of them would be off on sun-seeking, warm water Christmas and New Year cruises to the Caribbean. In reverse, the first days of January often witnessed a second gathering of these grand ships as they returned from their holiday voyages. Eight passenger liners are seen in this dramatic aerial view *(right, bottom)* dated December 1966. The *Atlantic* and the *Constitution* of American Export Lines are at the top; then there is United States Lines' *United States*; the *Empress of Canada*, Canadian Pacific; the *Queen Elizabeth* and *Franconia*, both Cunard; the *Queen Anna Maria*, Greek Line; and finally the *Brasil*, Moore-McCormack Lines.

Not all passenger liners berthed along Luxury Liner Row at those Upper West Side piers. The Norwegian America Line, as an example, used Pier 42, then Pier 45, and finally Pier 40, located down in Greenwich Village. The company ran a combination of transatlantic voyages to Copenhagen, Bergen, and Oslo, as well as many cruises. Here *(opposite, top)* we see the company's largest liners in 1962: the 18,700-ton, 878-passenger *Bergensfjord* on the left, and her running mate, the 16,800-ton, 646-berth *Oslofjord* on the right.

Known fondly as "the Spotless Fleet," the Holland America Line was in Hoboken for some ninety years, until they relocated to Lower Manhattan in 1963. It was especially difficult to lease a preferable city pier and so, like many others, the Dutch made do with a less convenient New Jersey facility. Dressed in flags for winter cruises, the *Maasdam* and the company flagship *Nieuw Amsterdam* share the Fifth Street pier in Hoboken *(opposite, bottom)*. Beyond are three freighters from Holland America, Irish Shipping Lines, and Chargeurs Reunis.

Up until the outbreak of the Second World War between 1939 and 1940, America maintained a separate fleet of small passenger liners, "the little liners" as Frank Braynard called them, that sailed in mostly coastal and Caribbean services. They offered frequent, convenient services to the likes of Portland, Norfolk, Miami, New

Orleans, Havana, and Vera Cruz. New York to Miami was priced from $65 in the late 1930s. Clyde Mallory Lines' *Iroquois*, seen here *(above)* passing Lower Manhattan, and her sister *Shawnee* were among the largest, best decorated small passenger ships, and even resembled the far larger, more important Atlantic liners with their twin funnels. The 6,200-ton *Iroquois* could carry up to 754 passengers.

Eastern Steamship Lines ran frequent services from their Lower Manhattan pier at Chambers Street to Boston, via the Cape Cod Canal, and also to Norfolk, Virginia. Steamers such as the 5,000-ton *Yarmouth* (*below*), "another mini ocean liner" according to Frank Braynard, carried as many as 750 passengers in first, as well as second class quarters, on overnight trips between New York and Boston. With daily sailings including Sunday, departures would be at 5:30 in the evening and arrival at 8:30 the following morning. Fares without a cabin berth in the late 1930s were $5, whereas cabins were $1 to $8 extra. Eastern's New York coastal service ended in 1941, as the Second World War intensified, and never resumed. In the 1950s, the 378-foot-long *Yarmouth* became a pioneer cruise ship from the infant port of Miami, today the busiest ocean liner port in the world.

After the Second World War, Moore-McCormack Lines used their pier at the foot of Canal Street for their three liners: the *Argentina*, *Brazil*, and *Uruguay*. Well known for their Friday afternoon sailings, they created a popular connection to Trinidad, Rio de Janeiro, Santos, Montevideo, and Buenos Aires, with the complete voyage taking 38 days. Here *(above)* we see the *Uruguay* passing under the Bayonne Bridge being towed by Moran tugs during her postwar refit in the fall of 1947. The refit began in a Brooklyn shipyard that went on strike, so the ship was moved across the Lower Bay and along Kill van Kull and into Newark Bay to the Federal Shipyards in Kearny, New Jersey for completion.

In the 1950s and '60s, Grace Line was also known for its Friday departures for tropic waters. The 1932-built sisters *Santa Paula* shown here *(below)* and *Santa Rosa* sailed, for example, each Friday at noon, bound on 12-day roundtrip voyages to Aruba, La Guaira, Curacao, and Cartagena. Designed by William Francis Gibbs, the noted marine architect, the ships were predecessors in ways to the larger *America* and to the superliner *United States* and, to some onlookers, there was a similarity between all four ships. After the Second World War, in the 1950s, the *Santa Paula* and her sister carried 225 all-first-class passengers.

A brand-new *Santa Rosa* and *Santa Paula* were commissioned in the summer of 1958 and replaced the earlier pair of the same name. They, too, were popular with their Friday departures, now revised slightly to 13-day itineraries that generally sailed from New York to Curacao, La Guaira, Aruba, Kingston, Port au Prince, and Port Everglades, Florida. In this busy scene of a Friday afternoon *(opposite, top)*, the 584-foot-long, 300-passenger *Santa Rosa* is being readied on the south side of Pier 57, at the foot of West 14th Street, for a typical Friday afternoon sailing. To the left are two Grace Line 52-berth combination passenger-cargo ships, the *Santa Monica*, seen on the far left, and the *Santa Luisa*. Also to the far left are three United States Lines' freighters and a Grace Line cargo ship. To the right, at Pier 56, is a small freighter and then the *Egda*, a Norwegian-flag cargo vessel operated by the Cosmopolitan Line.

Long established at the Chelsea Piers, the Grace Line relocated in 1968 and moved to innovative Pier 40 at the foot of West Houston Street in Greenwich Village. The pier, opened in March 1963, was initially built for the Holland America Line and their affiliate ships. Along with the Norwegian America Line, Grace subleased from the Dutch and shared the efficient, convenient three-berth terminal. In this April 1969 aerial view *(opposite, bottom)*, the *Santa Rosa* is in the foreground, the *Bergensfjord* is on the outer berth, and the *Rotterdam*, the Holland America Line flagship, is on the south side.

Israel's Zim Lines had to be content for some years with a passenger and cargo terminal along the East River, at a pier at Kent Street in Brooklyn's Greenpoint section. Created along with the State of Israel in 1948, Zim developed an Atlantic passenger service between Haifa, other Mediterranean ports, and New York through a West German reparations agreement that included the construction of new ships. It was supported by two, very modern passenger-cargo liners, the 313-passenger, two-class *Israel* and the *Zion* shown here *(above)* arriving at the bottom of the East River for the first time on March 23, 1956. At 9,500 tons each, they carried 313 passengers in first- and tourist-class quarters.

Between 1963 and '64, Grace Line added four unique passenger-cargo containerships for their weekly service to the west coast of South America. Because of their containerized cargoes, they required more specialized and spacious berths, and so used docks in rather distant Port Newark, New Jersey. The four modern sister ships, the *Santa Magdalena*, *Santa Maria*, *Santa Mariana* seen here arriving on her maiden call on June 20, 1963 *(right)*, and *Santa Mercedes*, also carried 125 passengers in luxurious, all-first-class quarters.

After the first commercial jet crossings on the Atlantic in October 1958, the Atlantic ocean liner trade began its gradual, but steady decline. Some ninety-five percent of all Atlantic travelers used airlines by 1963. The once popular, beloved, and very profitable liners grew desolate, dowdy, and certainly unprofitable. In the '60s, one by one drifted off into retirement. But perhaps the greatest symbol of the decline was the final departure of the 31-year-old *Queen Mary* in September 1967 *(opposite, top)*. Luxury liner of the '30s, speed queen, wartime trooper, and notably the last of the once familiar "three stackers," the money-losing *Mary* was, however, booked solid for that last crossing by mostly sentimental and nostalgic fans. While there were various proposals for her future, including the possibility of becoming a city high school moored along the Brooklyn waterfront, she went on to become a museum, hotel, and collection of onboard shops in southern California, in the distant waters of the port of Long Beach. The *Queen Elizabeth*, which had followed her into retirement thirteen months later, in October 1968, had a far less happy fate. While being refitted as a Chinese-owned, combination

floating university–cruise ship, she burned out and then capsized in Hong Kong harbor in January 1972. Her scorched, twisted remains had to be scrapped.

By the late 1970s, the West Side piers were primarily being used by a handful of cruise ships making increasingly popular weeklong jaunts to the Bahamas and Bermuda. With the exception of the *Queen Elizabeth 2*, the legendary ship also dubbed *QE2* and commissioned in May 1969, Atlantic sailings all but disappeared. During the cold winter months, when cruise liners themselves fled to warmer waters, the piers were all but idle for months at a time. One attempt at a year-round service for passengers, as well as their cars, was the introduction, in September 1982, of the 26,700-ton, 1,600-passenger, cruise ship–ferry *Scandinavia* *(opposite, bottom)*. She ran a steady service between New York and Freeport in the Bahamas and also transferred passengers and their cars to other vessels for short connections to Florida. Owned by the Danes, so-called Scandinavian World Cruises proved less than a great success and, within a year, the *Scandinavia* was reassigned and the New York service closed down.

Cruising out of New York grew more and more popular in the 1990s. Voyages ranged from one-night "party and gambling" trips to two weeks to New England and Eastern Canada. Expectedly, weekend departures were the more popular. The likes of mighty Carnival Cruise Lines, with 100,000-ton, 2,600-passenger ships, arrived by the late '90s and prompted even greater success. But for a time, a few older, veteran passenger ships continued on. Ships such as the 45-year-old *Regal Empress*, seen here *(left)* in August 1999, and the former *Olympia* of the Greek Line, which sailed for a one-ship operator, Florida-based Regal Cruises, but in summers from New York on 1 to 12 day itineraries. Older ships tended to signal lower prices and were therefore popular with families, groups, and conventions.

The last of the grand French liners, the *France*, left New York for the final time in September 1974. She was, however, reincarnated in 1980 as the cruise ship *Norway*. Her debut in May of that year, an Atlantic delivery voyage from Bremerhaven, Oslo, and Southampton, included an overnight call at Luxury Liner Row. Thereafter, she was based primarily in the booming Florida cruise trade, sailing weekly from Miami, now replacing New York as the biggest and busiest ocean liner port in the world, on weeklong voyages to the sunny Caribbean. The world's longest liner (1,035 feet overall) until the commissioning of the *Queen Mary 2* in late 2003 (at 1,132 feet), the *Norway* has returned to New York on occasion as part of periodic, refit-linked trips to and from Europe. She is seen here *(below)*, passing the World Trade Center on the afternoon of September 5, 2001.

CHAPTER FOUR
Serving the Fleet: Busy Harborcraft

Until as late as the early 1970s, New York harbor bustled with ships of every kind. It was like an ongoing performance of a long-running play. For those interested there was always something to see. Of course, there were the great liners, those "floating palaces" that were known by name, and even country and owner, by many. Many onlookers easily recognized the *Queen Mary*, the *United States*, the *Independence*, and the *Ile de France*. Then there were the freighters, romantic and intriguing vessels in their own right, hauling cargoes of every description to and from exotic ports in every corner of the globe. And there was an added magic to those charismatic tramp steamers, older, less identifiable, and sometimes well-worn craft that carried all sorts of cargo, from coal to scrap metal, grain, and used automobiles. Too, the harbor had its own fleet of ships; also greater "characters" in the ongoing production called "the port." There were the tugs, barges, floating cranes, ferries, fireboats, and specialty craft such as the big, boxy, brown-colored floating grain elevators.

"We used to say that the letter 'S' would get more use in describing the Port of New York in, say, the 1950s than any other letter," recalled the late Captain Fred Johnson, who worked aboard harbor tugs for some fifty years, until the mid-1970s. "Words like superb, superlative, sights, sounds, smells, ships, sails, significant, seamen, stupendous, and shrill vie for usage. But above all, it was statistics that really told the story of the harbor."

"Well, in the first place, the Port of New York laid claim to be the greatest port because it has frontage of some 550 miles on navigable waterways and measured along bulkheads," noted Captain Johnson. "There are 350 or so miles in New York and some 200 in New Jersey. That is taking advantage of the fact that eight large bays, Jamaica, Upper and Lower, Raritan, Gravesend, Newark, Flushing, and Eastchester are considered part of the port.

"Along Manhattan Island, for example, there was 38 miles of waterfront," he added, "and along Brooklyn's waterside there is 79 miles. One authority once pointed out that all the fleets in the world [1950] could be anchored in New York harbor's 175 square miles and with room to spare. There were times, incidentally, during and just after the Second World War, when it looked as if all the fleets of the world were anchored off New York!"

According to records, April 19, 1946 was the busiest day when 566 oceangoing ships were in port. In addition, there was a fleet of over 2,500 combined tugboats, barges, lighters, carfloats, and floating cranes that every day called New York their home port. Of the 566 vessels, it was also noted that 464 were American owned.

Port commerce continued to be tremendous for some years afterward. From July 1, 1949 until June 30, 1950, for example, 7,950 vessels entered the harbor, arriving from forty-two different countries, laden with 34,887,982 net tons of cargo. Clearing the harbor for the same period were 8,114 oceangoing ships carrying 35,433,751 net tons of freight. Altogether, it is a one-year total of 16,064 foreign-trade vessels entering or leaving with an aggregate tonnage of 70,321,733! In addition, more than 6,000 vessels in coastal and intracoastal trades entered and left the port. In all, New York harbor in 1950 handled more than forty-five percent of the nation's imports and exports measured in dollar value—five times that of the average for all other U.S. ports.

"I was very, very fortunate to have worked in the New York harbor of that era," concluded Captain Johnson. "It really was the greatest port anywhere in the world. It was something to behold and to know, and to be very proud of!"

The great tugboat companies had names such as Moran, McAllister, Dalzell, Meseck, Turecamo, and Red Star. There were 400 tugs in and around New York harbor just after World War II, in 1946. Here *(opposite, top)* we see the tug *Brian McAllister* doing a routine chore: she is docking a Danish freighter, the *Wyoming*, in a view dated May 14, 1964.

Prior to the age of supertankers and large container-cargo ships, handling the great ocean liners was considered the most demanding task. On her maiden arrival into New York harbor, on August 23, 1950, no less than eight tugs were used to berth the 936-foot-long *Liberte* of the French Line. The 51,000-ton luxury ship was then the third largest liner afloat, surpassed in size only by the 81,000-ton *Queen Mary* and the 83,000-ton *Queen Elizabeth*. "Tugs had far less power in the 1950s," commented James McNamara, "and so we see four on the bow of a big liner like the *Liberte*," *(opposite, bottom)*.

Rugged work: a tugboatman handles thick hemp lines on a summer's morning in this scene *(left)* in New York's Lower Bay. "To be a crewman on a tugboat in New York harbor in the 1950s and '60s was considered an excellent position," noted Captain McNamara. "The work was hard, the hours often long, but the salaries were very good."

Skillful work: a line is tight and fixed from the port side stern of the 53,000-ton superliner *United States (below),* as she begins yet another noontime departure from Manhattan's Pier 86.

Some of the greatest gatherings of harbor tugs were during maiden arrivals of the great liners. Here (*above*) in a view from February 1962, we see tugs from the likes of Moran, Dalzell, McAllister, Esso, and the United States Coast Guard as they form a gala escort to the longest liner yet built, the 1,035-foot-long *France*. The brand-new pride of the French Merchant Marine was arriving in New York for the first time and the occasion was high spirited.

To the rescue! Sometimes tugs and other harborcraft were called to emergency situations. This photo (*below*), dated June 27, 1950, is titled "Victims of Collision." The outbound American Export Lines' passenger-cargo ship *Excalibur* seen in the background carrying some 125 passengers and freight, had just left her Jersey City berth on a voyage to the Mediterranean when, in the Upper Bay, she collided with the Danish freighter *Colombia* in the foreground. The 5,100-ton *Colombia* has caught fire and is being moved to a Brooklyn pier while the 9,600-ton *Excalibur*, which started sinking by the bow following the collision, is being towed for beaching in 32 feet of water in the Red Hook Flats off Brooklyn. Both ships were later repaired.

Railroad tugs were plentiful in and around the port until the early 1970s. All of the great railway companies had them to look after their barges, lighters, floating cranes, and carfloats. There was Erie, Central Railroad of New Jersey, Baltimore & Ohio, Lackawanna, New York Central, the New York Dock Railway Company, and others. These tugs rarely, if ever, handled deep-sea ships, but instead looked after harborcraft. Pausing between weekday chores, we see in this photo (*above*) four New York Central Railroad tugs on a wintery Saturday afternoon at a dock in Weehawken, New Jersey.

"In ways, these railway tugs were the most traditional of their type in all of New York harbor. They were classics," noted James McNamara.

The large oil companies like Esso, Texaco, and Mobil maintained tugboat fleets as well. In this 1959 view (*below*), we see the tug *Socony 10* shifting fuel barges alongside the liner *Olympia*, flagship of the Greek Line. Berthed on the south side of Pier 88, the refueling would take 6 to 8 hours for a liner such as the 23,000-ton *Olympia*.

Oceangoing tugs were slightly larger, had different hull shapes, and were more powerful than ordinary harbor tugs. Here *(above)* we see Moran's *Eugenia M. Moran* in the Upper Bay, just off Lower Manhattan. "The big, C4-class freighter *Mount Greylock* was used in American President Line's around-the-world service until the early 1950s," added Captain McNamara. "In this view, I suspect that she is going to Todd's shipyard in Erie Basin and then to lay up, perhaps in the James River in Virginia.

"Dispatchers at Moran Towing could sometimes keep an eye on things from the 25th floor balcony of the company's offices at 17 Battery Place," noted Captain McNamara. "Back in the 1930s, the dispatchers used to bark orders through megaphones to waiting tugs, but it had all changed to radio microphones by the '50s." In this case, however, Admiral Eugene F. Moran is watching his tugs at work *(left)*, this one undocking United Fruit's *Choluteca*. Another United Fruit ship, the *Cape Cod*, is to the right, and a Central Railroad of New Jersey ferry, the *Westfield*, is in mid-river on her relays between Liberty Street in Lower Manhattan and the Railroad's terminal at Johnson Avenue, Jersey City.

The Erie Railroad tug *Paterson* delivers an open freight barge with very little aboard to the *Ciudad de Barranquilla* (**above**), a freighter belonging to Grancolombiana and berthed in Brooklyn Heights. "Some veteran New York harborcraft live on. The *Paterson*, for example, is still about [2004], still at work, but under a different name and in New Orleans," added Captain McNamara.

Moving cargo on barges was a brisk business. In the fading afternoon light of a winter's day, a Moran tug pushes a coal barge after having just passed under the Manhattan Bridge on the East River (**below**). The Lower Manhattan skyline is in the background. "The tug is pushing this coal barge to a power plant, perhaps to a destination further along the East River or at Hell Gate or even out to Long Island," noted Captain McNamara. "Most likely, it would have been loaded in the Kills [Kill van Kull] by 'coal tipplers' [coal-loading machines]."

Merritt-Chapman & Scott Corporation, a harbor company dating from 1860, were specialists in both salvage and heavy-lift operations. Their floating cranes busily served the harbor's bulk cargo needs, often being moored directly alongside docked deep-sea ships. The steam-powered *Century*, with a lifting capacity of 250 tons, is seen here *(opposite, top)* in this 1950s view off-loading heavy equipment at the Todd Shipyards in Erie Basin, Brooklyn. She and her sister, the *Monarch*, were the mightiest floating cranes in the port in their day.

Here *(opposite, middle)*, in a 1959 photograph, at the Kent Street pier in the Greenpoint section of Brooklyn, the *Constellation* handles heavy-lift items bound for the Mediterranean. The items themselves have arrived aboard Lackawanna railway carfloats. "Although one of the smaller, less powerful in the Merritt-Chapman fleet, this floating crane is actually loading other cranes aboard the *Israel* of Zim Lines," noted Captain McNamara. "The booms and buckets are on deck while the crane cabs, which are 50 tons each, are waiting on the barge."

Floating cranes came in varied forms and creations. Here at the Central Railroad of New Jersey piers in Jersey City, two floating "goose neck" cranes are off-loading cargo from Africa *(opposite, bottom)*. The large freighter on the left is the *Sea Falcon* while the Liberty ship *Edward W. Bok* is docked behind her. "This big, C-3 class freighter is actually on charter to the Farrell Lines. It is just after the Second World War, in about 1946, and she is Ingalls-built [Ingalls Shipbuilding Corporation in Pascagoula, Mississippi] because of the noticeable corrugated deckhouse," said Captain McNamara.

A festive occasion! New York harbor fireboats, such as the *John J. Harvey*, often helped in welcoming new ships with streams of sprouting water. Seen here *(above)* off Lower Manhattan, in 1951, the brand-new Argentine State Line combination passenger-cargo liner *Rio Jachal*, built in Italy for the New York–Buenos Aires trade, is escorted to her Franklin Street pier. The 1935-built *Harvey* is today a museum and occasionally still makes excursions around the harbor. She is based near the Chelsea Docks, at Pier 63.

Fires aboard ships in port are worrisome. They can often spread to the dock itself. Just prior to sailing for Europe from Pier 84, at West 44th Street, the Hamburg Atlantic Line's 30,000-ton liner *Hanseatic* caught fire in September 1966 *(above)*. She was quickly evacuated of passengers and most crewmembers, and the fireboats, Coast Guard craft, and tugs hurried to the scene. While the blaze was eventually extinguished, her voyage was canceled and the 672-foot-long ship towed to the Todd Shipyard in Erie Basin, Brooklyn for inspection and evaluation for repair. Unfortunately, the smell of smoke had permeated throughout the 36-year-old vessel's luxurious interiors. Expensive repair costs against her age were far too great and so she was towed across the North Atlantic to Hamburg and then scrapped there. "It was the smell of smoke that finished off the

Hanseatic. It was not the fire damage," recalled the late Captain Joseph Mazzotta of the United States Coast Guard.

Fires at night in the port could be even more difficult. On a warm night in September 1962, at Pier 25, at the foot of Franklin Street in Lower Manhattan, the 11,000-ton *Rio de la Plata* of the Argentine State Line caught fire *(below)*. Again, and along with other craft, the fireboat *John J. Harvey* was called to battle the blaze aboard the 550-foot-long ship that was due to sail to ports along the east coast of South America. She too was taken to Todd's in Brooklyn. The repairs deemed too expensive, and so she was laid up at an otherwise unused Brooklyn pier until April 1964, then returned to Buenos Aires only to burn again in April 1968 and then to be scrapped two years later.

CHAPTER FIVE
Shipshape Condition: The Bustling Shipyards

A peninsular juts out from Bayonne; the New Jersey community just across Kill van Kull, north of Staten Island facing onto the Lower Bay. Back at the beginning of the Second World War, in 1941, the U.S. Navy wanted to build an additional repair facility within New York harbor, a sort of adjunct to the huge naval shipyard over in Brooklyn, which had one handicap for bigger warships: they needed to pass under the low-lying Brooklyn and Manhattan bridges on the East River. And so, a 1,100-foot-long graving dock was built in Bayonne, repair facilities added, workshops built, and four heavy-lift cranes installed (two of them were among the tallest in the port).

Expectedly, work at Bayonne was always hectic during the urgent war years. Along with battleships, heavy cruisers, and some of the early aircraft carriers, the world's largest passenger liners, which were then the world's biggest troopships, the gray-painted *Queen Mary* and *Queen Elizabeth*, put into the Bayonne graving dock for quick repairs and maintenance. In late 1943, the salvaged hull of the 83,000-ton *Normandie* was inspected briefly there as well, before being sent over to the Columbia Street pier in Brooklyn to await her postwar fate. In 1945, as the war ended, another liner-trooper, in fact, then the third largest ship afloat, the former German *Europa* was also handled at Bayonne.

Bayonne's postwar work was almost as plentiful. Along with the Brooklyn Navy Yard (also known as the New York Naval Shipyard), there were six other large ship repair facilities in New York harbor. Bethlehem Steel had four: 27th Street and 56th Street plants in Brooklyn, one in Hoboken, and another (which also did some ship construction) on the north shore of Staten Island. Todd had two shipyards: one in the Eire Basin in Brooklyn and the other also in Hoboken.

Until the early 1970s, it was mostly light military work that kept the Bayonne facility (commonly referred to as the Bayonne Navy Yard) going. It was especially busy with preparing decommissioned warships for the "mothball fleets" or, in times of government and military downsizing, for the scrappers. The speed queen *United States* made three quick calls to the graving dock in the 1950s, but always under extra-tight security (because of her highly classified underwater hull design). Her running mate, the smaller *America*, called, as well.

By the mid-1970s, however, the Navy was gradually pulling out of Bayonne and the repair portion of the facility was leased to Bethlehem Steel, who wanted to be prepared to handle bigger ships in the increasingly competitive ship repair trades. There were freighters, tankers, large containerships, and ocean liners such as the *Queen Elizabeth 2*, *Oceanic*, *Doric*, *Emerald Seas*, and the revived *America*, which had been sailing for some years as the Greek *Australis*. But Bethlehem Steel pulled out, as well, in 1982, and after a brief reprieve as part of the Braswell shipyard, Bayonne closed down altogether. The great graving dock became weed-infested and neglected. It seemed to be the fate of New York harbor shipyards. All of the other Bethlehem Steel shipyards were closed, as well, with the Hoboken facility being demolished and rebuilt as luxury housing. Todd's Hoboken plant had a similar fate, but was resurrected for offices, a marina, and restaurants.

In October 2002, after being refitted and upgraded, the so-called Bayonne Shipyard, an arm of the Coastal Shipyard, which leases space in the former Brooklyn Navy Yard, opened for business. One of the aims of the new operators is to do cruise ship repairs and refits.

A large peninsular jutting out from Bayonne, New Jersey into the Lower Bay included a large graving dock, built in 1942, capable of handling the largest ships afloat. Used mostly by military and military-related ships, commercial ships occasionally put in for quick, often urgent repairs. Here *(right, top)*, in a view from July 19, 1954, the superliner *United States* needed adjustments to her propellers, a job that needed to be hurriedly scheduled between her arrival from Europe that same morning and then her return departure in five days, on the 24th. The 990-foot-long liner is being carefully guided into position before the dock is drained of water. According to Captain McNamara, "The graving dock at Bayonne was built especially for battleships. Today, it would make a great container pier with cranes along both sides."

The Bethlehem Steel Company had four shipyards in the Port of New York until the early 1960s. Altogether, there were eighteen dry docks, four shipbuilding ways (at their Staten Island plant), and the equivalent of five miles of berthing space. The largest facility was their Hoboken plant, which, by 1960, had five docks, four floating dry docks, and seven cranes. Hoboken, which employed up to 11,000 workers during the Second World War, also had tank-cleaning facilities, two oil-cleaning tugs and storage barges, three modern work boats (for dockside repairs), and was noted in being one of the world's finest marine engine repair yards. In this view *(right, bottom)* from 1955, we see United Fruit's 7,600-ton *Heredia*, normally on the Caribbean "banana boat" run, in one of the floating docks and, among other work, is having her rudder cleaned and painted. "Bethlehem Steel had an excellent reputation in its day. They provided the finest in repairs and ship maintenance," said Captain McNamara. "My whole family worked in the Hoboken yard, including my mother at one time or another."

When the Grace Line retired their veteran, 1932-built *Santa Paula* in June 1958, she was replaced by the brand-new *Santa Rosa*. The *Santa Paula*'s sister, the *Santa Rosa*, would remain in service, however, for three months, and was renamed *Santa Paula*. Then, in September, when the new *Santa Paula* was commissioned, the older *Santa Paula* (ex-*Santa Rosa*) was retired, as well. The two older ships, both named *Santa Paula*, were laid up at the Bethlehem yard in Hoboken, and remained there for some three years, until sold in 1961 to become Greek cruise ships. In this view *(right)* at Hoboken, dated January 26, 1959, the *Santa Paula* and the "other" *Santa Paula* (ex-*Santa Rosa*) are moored together for de-storing and decommissioning. Later, the two ships were nested alongside one another.

A demanding job for Bethlehem's Hoboken yard came in March 1959 when the Norwegian tanker *Jalanta* was cut in two by the inbound liner *Constitution* just outside the Narrows *(below)*. The tanker and her severed bow section were saved; both later brought to Hoboken and then, with repairs, reattached. The 12,200-ton *Jalanta* was again sailing that summer. "The *Jalanta* was a rather unique repair job for its time since they were able to save both parts and rejoin them," noted Captain McNamara.

Just north of the Bethlehem Steel Shipyard in Hoboken was the another large ship repair facility, this one belonging to Todd Shipyards *(left)*. There were three large floating docks, a large machine shop, and special capabilities with smaller vessels. It was busy until the early 1960s and then, through consolidation, combined with Todd's Erie Basin facility. The Hoboken yard was closed in 1965 and later rebuilt as a hotel, office complex, and marina. "That great, lighted sign facing the Hudson and toward Manhattan said it all," noted Captain McNamara. "It represented a fine, busy shipyard in the heyday of the Port of New York."

Todd's flagship shipyard in New York harbor was located in Erie Basin in Brooklyn. In this view *(below)* dated October 25, 1935, the effects of a September hurricane in the Caribbean were brought closer to home. The Holland America liner *Rotterdam*, which was blown ashore during a cruise off Kingston, Jamaica, and the Morgan Line's coastal passenger ship *Dixie*, which grounded on a reef off the Florida coast, are in for repairs. While damage to the 24,100-ton *Rotterdam* was less extensive, repairs to the 8,100-ton *Dixie* would cost $400,000 and take ten months. "It is interesting to note how underdeveloped and shabby the area around the shipyard is in this 1930s, Depression era view," added Captain McNamara. "The graving dock being used by the *Rotterdam* [697-feet long] is the oldest dock of its kind in all of New York harbor. It dates from the Civil War period. It was put to one of its greatest tests when another Holland America liner, the *Nieuw Amsterdam* [758 feet long], used it in 1940. Evidently, there were only inches to spare."

The 441-foot-long, Greek-flag Liberty ship *Hellenic Beach* lost her bow in a predawn collision in the Delaware River and then limped to her Brooklyn pier. Afterward, the Hellenic Lines' ship was moved to the Todd Shipyard in Erie Basin, where this photograph (*left*) was taken on June 11, 1949. The "plastic surgery," as Todd officials called it, was completed in four days. "Repairing a bow, especially on a prefab ship such as a Liberty, was not as hard or as difficult as it seems," added Captain McNamara.

Todd's Erie Basin yard was kept busy well into the 1970s. Work began to decline as shipowners instead sought out less expensive foreign yards when this photo (*below*) was taken in 1974. A Texaco tanker is on the far left, and then the burned-out hull of the containership *Sea Witch*, which belonged to American Export Isbrandtsen Lines caught fire following a collision with an Esso tanker practically under the Verrazano-Narrows Bridge in June 1973. In the center, there is a tanker and one of the Prudential Lines' freighters, the *Santa Elena*, in the floating dock.

Bethlehem Steel had two plants along the Brooklyn waterfront, one at 27th Street and the other at 56th Street. The latter was the busier, handling the likes of big ocean liners such as the 30,000-ton sisters *Independence* and *Constitution*. "The largest floating dock in New York was, for many years and until the early '60s, at Bethlehem Steel's 56th Street yard in Brooklyn," noted Captain McNamara. "Here *(above)* we see three troopships at dock plus an Isbrandtsen Line freighter on the left. It might seem tight, but it was actually very easy to move and shift vessels, which often happened in busy shipyard settings. Ships often came for short periods, sometimes just overnight to get steam for their generators or light welding. New York shipyards were always slightly more expensive, but they were conveniently located and usually fast."

Most ships seemed far bigger when out of water and in a floating dock, especially at night when they would be floodlit. The big floating dock at Bethlehem Steel's 56th Street yard in Brooklyn is seen here *(opposite, top)* during the Second World War, on June 23, 1942. The 8,000-capacity troopship *Monterey*, a Matson Line passenger ship used in peacetime Pacific service, is taking a quick break from her urgent wartime duties for repairs to her propellers. Officially, the work to the 18,000-ton former luxury liner was listed as "voyage repairs."

A taxing job for Bethlehem's 56th Street yard came in July 1956. After colliding with the Italian liner *Andrea Doria*, the 12,000-ton Swedish American liner *Stockholm* returned to New York minus her bow *(opposite, bottom)*. After off-loading her passengers, survivors from the *Doria* and most of crew, the 525-foot-long ship was handed over to Bethlehem and given a new bow. She resumed sailing that December.

After the Brooklyn Naval Shipyard closed down in 1971, the Seatrain Lines, noted for their railway car–carrying ships, formed an offshoot, the Seatrain Shipbuilding Corporation. Seatrain leased part of the large naval facility for repairs, as well as for building ships, one of which was another supertanker, thoughtfully named *Brooklyn* in 1973. One customer was the 70,000-ton supertanker *Manhattan*, which had been fitted with a special bow for Northwest Passage voyages. The 875-foot-long ship is seen here

(above), being looked after by several Moran tugs as she passes under the Manhattan Bridge. Using a high-powered zoom lens, this photo was taken from the 53rd floor of 1 World Trade Center.

Owned by United States Steel, the Federal Shipbuilding & Dry Dock Company, located in Kearny, New Jersey, about ten miles west of Manhattan, reached its peak during the Second World War when it churned out some 400 ships. But after the war ended, between 1946 and '47, the yard had few shipbuilding prospects and so was reinvented as a shipbreaking yard. Until 1989, the plant, under the name of the Lipsett Corporation, demolished several hundred other vessels, many of them veterans of the World War II service. "In its day, Federal in Kearny was one of the best shipyards anywhere," noted James McNamara. "It later turned into one of the busiest scrapyards, dismantling the likes of the famed aircraft carrier *Enterprise*, many liners such as the *Washington* and *Manhattan* and scores of freighters. Here *(left)* in this view [from January 1973], we see the *Walter F. Perry*, a modified Liberty with heavy-lift gear. Her all-white hull tells us that she was used as a grain storage in later years. The light coloring reflected the sun and so there was less onboard heating to disturb the grain."

CHAPTER SIX
In Gray Paint: The Military Fleet

"I had a perfect, but very saddening view of the great *Normandie* when she burned along New York's West Side waterfront on a cold afternoon in February 1942. Smoke poured over midtown Manhattan. It was orange-brown color," recalled Harold Oshzy, who worked at the time on the 28th floor of the RKO Building in Rockefeller Center. The *Normandie* fire was a dramatic, well-remembered notation as New York harbor went to war in the early 1940s. Not at sea or in foreign ports by enemy subs or air-craft, one of the three largest Allied troopships was in fact lost in the very confines of New York harbor. To many, it was one of the war's saddest moments. For Oshzy, it also seemed to start a long association with ocean liners that later included forty-four Atlantic crossings, and well over fifty cruises. "I saw the *Normandie* blazing and then, the next day, saw the ship on its side. She was still sizzling, liked the doomed creature she was. It was a sad view of a great ship."

Jack Watson also recalled the dark days of the Second World War in New York and the burning of the *Normandie*. "I was a young, assistant photographer for the *New York Daily News* and was sent over to the West Side on the night of February 9, 1942. My assignment was to help cover the big fire that day aboard the grand French luxury liner *Normandie*. But by 10th Avenue, I found I could not get within two blocks of the ship, which was on the north side of Pier 88, at West 48th Street. A cordon of U.S. Army soldiers stood in tight guard around the area. The ship was, after all, government property and was being converted to a Navy troop transport at the time. We stood and waited, but made no progress. It seemed that there would be no photographs. But at about 2:00 in the morning, a great sound—a big swish actually—filled the otherwise quiet night. Overloaded with firefighters' water, the *Normandie* rolled over and capsized on her side."

"The soldiers turned and some began to walk toward Pier 88, and so left openings for the press to get through," added Watson. "I saw the ship on her side, a huge, dead monster, still creaking and moaning. Streams of smoke and steam rose in the cold night sky as the hot steel hit the icy waters of the Hudson River. It was an incredible sight! It was also an emotional one. One of the world's greatest and most famous and popular ships was almost certainly lost, a dead cause to the war effort and to any future she might have had as a peacetime ocean liner. And our spirits were already low since the attack on Pearl Harbor had occurred only two months before."

World War II for America and for the Port of New York had already started and when Harold Oshzy left the comforts of his midtown office for the cramped bunks aboard the trooper *Aquitania*, the converted Cunard liner. Along with 9,000 others, he left Pier 90 (just a block or so north of the capsized, gutted *Normandie*) in 1943. "The *Aquitania* was an 'old tub.' She was already nearly thirty years old. Everything onboard moaned and rattled," he recalled. "She had four tall stacks [the last afloat with that number, in fact] and lots of cluttered ventilators, wind scoops and pipes. She was an old girl, both inside and out. But she was still fast, about 23 knots at top speed, and could outrun the Nazi subs. We zigzagged all the way and, of course, sailed completely blacked-out at night. Every one of the troops was sick, or so it seemed. The *Aquitania* rolled terribly. Actually, being sick was a daily activity. The smell of kippers coming out of the British officers' dining room actually made everyone even sicker. I was in a tiny stateroom stacked high with canvas bunks. Some of the GI's wanted 'extra submarine pay' because their cabins and bunks were below the waterline. It was a great relief to finally drop anchor at Greenock in Scotland and go ashore."

Two years later, in the summer of 1945, Oshzy's return to the states was quite different. The six days on the *Aquitania* became sixteen days on a much smaller, far slower Victory ship, which had been made over as a troop transport. "It was a longer, much more tedious trip home from Europe on the *Wooster Victory*," he recalled. "It seemed endless. We hit a violent storm just outside the wide entrance to New York harbor. Two days later, we found ourselves off Portland, Maine. But when we returned to New York, we were actually disappointed that there wasn't a bigger wel-come as we passed through the Narrows. It seemed at first that no one bothered. But then, as we moved up the Lower Bay toward Manhattan, a great commotion erupted. Suddenly, there were horns, a spraying fireboat, waving flags, an overhead blimp, and friendly waves from ferryboats. Tugboats formed an escort. Ladies came aboard the *Wooster Victory* at Pier 84 with donuts and real milk. What a day! What a grand welcome! The war was over!"

York–Bermuda cruise run, the 22,500-ton *Monarch of Bermuda* is seen here *(opposite, bottom)*, temporarily docked at the Bush Terminal in Brooklyn awaiting her call to duty.

While most liners were eventually converted for wartime troop transport services, two of them found more unusual duties. Sweden's *Gripsholm* and a running mate, the *Drottningholm*, were used as so-called Diplomatic Exchange Ships, sailing in neutral status with diplomats and government officials, refugees, displaced persons, prisoners, and some wounded. The two ships free of attack, traveled to ports around the world. "In this view *(left)* dated June 1943, New York harbor was congested with ships, many of them being marshaled for the great North Atlantic convoys," noted James McNamara. "And so, the *Gripsholm*, which was making irregular sailings as a neutral-flag exchange ship, was put 'out of harm's way' and moored up along the Hudson River off Yonkers for a time."

There were some tense moments for many otherwise familiar, friendly ships of New York harbor. In the first months of the war, some ships such as the Norwegian America Line's *Bergensfjord* continued to make her New York–Copenhagen–Oslo sailings. Her then neutral status was clearly noted by the markings along her sides. However, in this scene *(below)* from March 17, 1940, the 11,000-ton passenger ship has been detained from sailing by U.S. Customs. It seems that her captain refused to carry any American mail bound for Europe and so the vessel was detained for a time at a Brooklyn Heights pier. The *Bergensfjord*, which had been sailing to New York since 1913, returned after the war, but as the *Argentina* of the Home Lines and later as the *Jerusalem* of the Zim Lines, the first large liner in the Israeli Merchant Marine.

PREPARATIONS FOR WAR. It is September 1939 and the French luxury liner *Champlain* is loading Caterpillar tanks for use by the French army *(opposite, top)*. When war was officially declared on September 3, many commercial liner sailngs were cancelled, curtailed, or disrupted. Inbound to New York, many passenger ships carried worried tourists, refugees, and Europeans fortunate enough to leave the troubled continent. The 28,200-ton *Champlain* was herself an early casualty of the hostilities, being mined and sunk off western France in June 1940.

Some noted passenger ships, such as Furness-Bermuda Line's *Monarch of Bermuda*, quickly lost their more festive commercial colors in the first days of the war, in September 1939, and were repainted in drab military grays. Normally on the New

One of Cunard's greatest and grandest liners, the 45,600-ton *Aquitania*, seen here *(above)* outbound in the Hudson River on September 23, 1939, continued to make some New York–Southampton sailings in that otherwise tense autumn of 1939. She was, however, repainted entirely in gray by this time and was carrying few eastbound passengers, but was booked to absolute capacity on the returns to the safe waters of America. Historically, by World War II, the *Aquitania* was the last of the four-funnel ocean liners.

Manhattan's West Side piers became increasingly important as the war started. Berthing space was often at a premium and so liners such as the *Ile de France*, laid up because of the uncertainty of events in her native France, sat idle at the French Line terminal at Pier 88 for a time. But the berth was soon needed and, in this view *(opposite, top)* dated November 23, 1939, the legendary 43,000-ton liner, then one of the world's largest and most luxurious, made an unusual, but short voyage. She was moved to a less important pier in Staten Island to await her wartime assignment. In fact, in March 1940, under Allied command, she sailed off to war, a large troopship traveling to the far corners of the world.

Cunard's second largest superliner, the 83,673-ton *Queen Elizabeth*, had been scheduled for a gala, flag-bedecked, commercial maiden voyage to New York in April 1940 *(opposite, bottom)*. Together with her running mate *Queen Mary*, it would also be the start of the world's first twin-liner express service on the Atlantic. The war changed everything, however, and instead the new *Elizabeth*, also the world's longest liner at 1,031 feet from stem to stern, sat incomplete at the shipyard in Clydebank, Scotland where she was built. But in February 1940, amidst rumors of sabotage or attack, she was ordered away, to the safety of America. Quickly, she fled, still incomplete in ways, but then arrived to a less enthusiastic maiden call at New York on March 7, 1940. Because of her speed and the top-secret urgency of that crossing, she was dubbed the "gray ghost." She docked at Pier 90, joining the already laid up *Queen Mary* and *Normandie*.

Sensibly, the French laid up the grand, 83,000-ton *Normandie* at Pier 88 from the end of August 1939 *(above)*. The North Atlantic was deemed unsafe and the future of France itself in uncertainty. Sadly, one of the greatest and grandest of all superliners would never put to sea again. With her 1,200 crew reduced to as few as one hundred maintenance and security staff, she remained at her berth for nearly two and a half years. "The three freighters laid up on the south side of Pier 88 had been purchased by the government from private owners. Through the Maritime Administration, the government had taken control of the West Side piers. It was the period of the so-called 'phony war' and these freighters, with their hatches closed and booms nested, were awaiting a call to duty," noted Captain McNamara.

Almost immediately after the attack on Pearl Harbor on December 7, 1941, and America's official entry in the Second World War on the 8th, the great *Normandie* was seized by the U.S. Government, assigned to the Department of the Navy and was renamed USS *Lafayette (below)*. She was to be converted, with over 15,000 berths, into one of the world's three largest Allied troopships, with the others being the *Queen Mary* and *Queen Elizabeth*.

One of the greatest tragedies of the entire war was the loss of the brilliant *Normandie*. While being stripped of her passenger ship finery and converted to a high-capacity, military trooper at Pier 88, sparks from a welder's acetylene torch ignited a fire that spread quickly over much of the 1,028-foot-long hull. Smoke streamed eastward, across midtown Manhattan, on that cold winter afternoon *(above)*.

The smoke increased on that afternoon and created an orange-brown haze as far off as Queens *(below)*. Afternoon and evening newspapers had bold headlines: "*Normandie* Burning!" Thousands flocked to the West Side, but were stopped at 10th Avenue. The fire and firefighting were said to be military operations under wartime security protection. "The burning and capsizing of the *Normandie* was a case of confusion and bureaucracy," according to Captain McNamara. "It was a true embarrassment for the New York City Fire Department."

As the fire continued well into the night of February 9, fireboats poured more and more water on the liner. Overloaded, she finally capsized, rolling over on her port side. She was not a complete loss, however. In this view *(left)*, taken on the following morning and with her still smoldering hulk encrusted in winter ice, the *Normandie* is much like a beached, dead whale.

Salvaging the *Normandie* was the greatest effort of its kind to date and cost a staggering $5 million. The upper half of the ship had to be removed in the process and then the ship was slowly pumped out and righted. Used as a U.S. Navy salvage school, work continued around the clock as seen in this nighttime view *(below)* at the foot of West 48th Street.

Once she was righted, the scarred, rusted *Normandie* was towed from Pier 88 and, after a brief inspection in the graving dock at Bayonne, New Jersey, was laid up for the duration of the war at the Columbia Street pier in Brooklyn. While there was some talk of possibly rebuilding her as a cut-down, smaller passenger ship, she was declared surplus by the U.S. Government and sold for scrap for $161,000 to the Lipsett Corporation. In this sad view (*above*), dated December 6, 1946, the remains of the French flagship, her name faintly visible in ghostly letters, passes under the Bayonne Bridge on her way to the scrappers at Port Newark.

Millions of troops passed through New York harbor during the Second World War. The greatest single number, 16,683 in all, departed aboard the *Queen Mary* in July 1943. Here (*below*) we see the return of servicemen in 1945 arriving aboard the USS *John Ericsson*, the former Swedish American liner *Kungsholm*.

Wartime freighters appeared in New York harbor by the thousands. Here *(above)* we see the *Fort McLoughlin*, with mounted guns fore and aft, southbound along the East River, on a voyage from New Haven to New York. Most likely, she then sailed for Europe.

The gray-painted Liberty ship *E. G. Hall* is seen here *(below)* docked at the Chelsea Piers and loading cargo for war-torn Europe. In 1943, New York harbor was said to be the "busiest port in the world." The freight in some 430,000 boxcars were unloaded and sent to ships. There were 500 tugs, 55 large floating cranes, 1,200 open barges, 900 closed barges, over 300 railway carfloats, and 75 floating grain elevators.

Repairs and refits were urgent during the war and shipyard crews often worked around the clock and seven days a week. Here at Bethlehem Steel's 56th Street yard in Brooklyn, the troopship *Monterey* is seen *(opposite, top)* in June 1942 undergoing repairs.

A SAFE RETURN. Swedish American Line's *Drottningholm* docks at Jersey City on June 1, 1942 with some of her 908 passengers lining the rails *(opposite, bottom)*. They look across to anxious friends and relatives. The liner, in diplomatic exchange service, brought diplomats, newspaper reporters, and stranded Americans on an attack-free voyage from Lisbon.

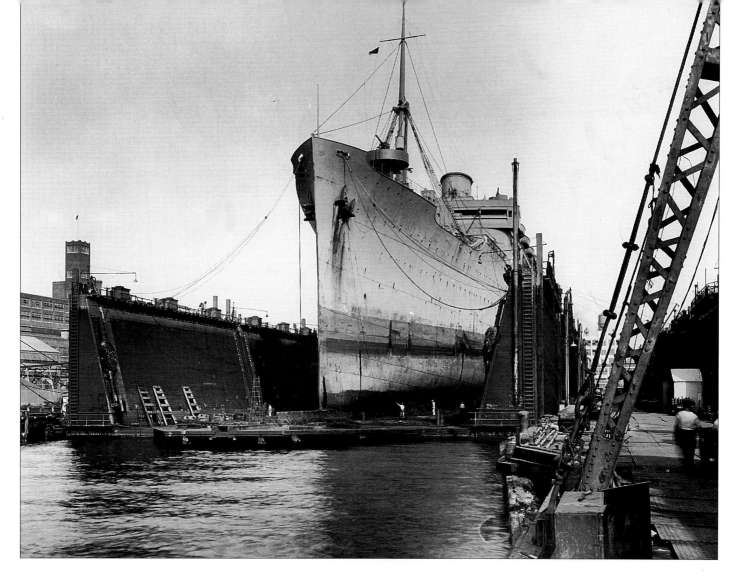

The most famous troopships of the war at New York harbor were the Cunard liners *Queen Mary*, seen here (**above**) on January 3, 1946, and *Queen Elizabeth*. Between January 1942 and the fall of 1945, the two Cunarders alone handled over two million service personnel. They operated in tandem, crossing in top secret between New York and Gourock, Scotland, largely in preparation of the Allied invasion of Europe. They left Pier 90, unannounced and usually in the cloak of night, zigzagged once at sea, and maintained lights out and radio silence all the way. Hitler had offered a large reward to the U-boat commander that would sink one of them, but their 30-knot-plus speeds gave them an added advantage.

Getting ships, especially passenger liners, back into shape for peacetime service was in itself a huge task at the Port of New York. Here (**below**) we see two prewar liners, the *George Washington* on the left and the *Argentina* on the right, undergoing postwar refits at the Bethlehem Steel Shipyard at 56th Street in Brooklyn. The 1908-built *George Washington* had actually served in the First World War, as well, while the *Argentina* had been the *Pennsylvania*, first commissioned in 1929. "It was an incredibly busy period with the revival and restoration of so many ships changing from war to peace," noted Captain McNamara.

North German Lloyd's *Europa* last visited New York in August 1939, still on the luxury run between New York and northern Europe. Kept in home waters by the Nazis, she was discovered lying and rusting at Bremerhaven by the invading American forces in May 1945, and was soon reconditioned as the troopship USS *Europa*. She returned to New York that September and was refitted as a postwar trooper at Hoboken and Bayonne. She is seen here *(above)*, on November 8, 1946, being docked at Pier 88 and in sight of the guns of the battleship USS *Missouri*. She departed for Southampton soon afterward and began her new duty: bringing Yankee servicemen home from war. While her prewar capacity was for 2,024 passengers, her new troop capacity was listed as 6,500.

Troop transports and other ships continued to bring servicemen, displaced persons, refugees, and even the last inmates of the Nazi death camps to New York until as late as the early 1950s. In a scene dated November 1, 1946 *(below)*, we see the 12,000-ton transport *General C. H. Muir* arriving at Pier 84 with 3,000 aboard. There were many joyous reunions along New York harbor piers in those years.

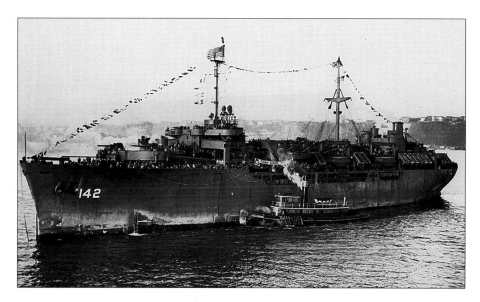

The famed, mighty Brooklyn Navy Yard was very busy during the war years. Formed on a small property in 1801, the facility grew to employ some 71,000 workers during its peak in the Second World War. Between 1941 and 1945, the yard reportedly repaired or overhauled no less than 5,000 ships, as well as constructing several hundred. In this view (*opposite, top*), dated December 11, 1944, we see one of the yard's most powerful symbols: the great hammerhead heavy-lift crane with a smaller satellite crane on top. It served the fleet until the mid-1960s. In the foreground, construction has begun on a new aircraft carrier, the 963-foot-long USS *Franklin D. Roosevelt*.

Another happy occasion for the "Can Do Yard," as the Brooklyn Navy Yard was dubbed. The supercarrier USS *Saratoga* is being readied for commissioning in this April 1956 photo (*opposite, bottom*). The Williamsburg Bridge is just behind.

Military ships on goodwill, open-house visits have proved very popular to this day. In this scene (*above*) from the early 1960s, the carrier USS *Wasp* sails along the lower Hudson en route to a berth in midtown for public inspection.

After the war and until the early 1970s, among other military ships, the U.S. Government maintained a fleet of gray-painted troopships. They often came and went from the Brooklyn Army Terminal, carrying peacetime troops, as well as dependant families. When the government turned completely to air transport, however, these mostly wartime-built troopships such as the *General Alexander M. Patch*, seen here (*left*) departing from the Todd shipyard in Brooklyn's Erie Basin, were dispatched to the "mothball fleets" in Virginia.

CHAPTER SEVEN
Changing Face: A Different Port

Famed ocean liners such as the *Albert Ballin*, the *Reliance*, and the *St. Louis* once docked there. Later, after the Second World War, there were liners such as the *Independence*, the *Saturnia*, and the infamous *Andrea Doria*. Closed since 1974, largely demolished, and reduced to a single level, Manhattan's Pier 84 is, as of the summer of 2004, coming back to life, but for far different kinds of "boats," if you will. Covered by a tensile covering, the pier is being revived as a student-training center for the building, repair, and operation of small boats. It is all part of a city program called "Floating the Apple."

Rebuilding and reviving Pier 84 is part of the enormous changes that have taken place in New York harbor in recent years. After years of abandonment and the inevitable decay and ruin, many of the facilities seen in the pages of this book, while part of a glorious, commercial maritime era, have fallen victim to the wrecking ball. In general, the waterfront is now for people, pleasure, and participation. Gone are the days when it was generally regarded with distance, even avoidance, the gritty waterside docks and warehouses, the ships and their seamen. The port has been renewed with great success and there is more to come, new developments and projects that will see the light of day long after this book is published.

Located at the foot of West 44th Street and just south of the popular USS *Intrepid* Air & Space Museum, Pier 84 was built by the city's then Department of Marine Terminals back in 1926. Its first and only tenant was the Hamburg America Line, one of the greatest German shipowners, which ran, among many others, four big passenger-cargo liners on the Hamburg–New York route. They were the aforementioned *Albert Ballin* and her sisters and near-sisters, the *Deutschland*, the *Hamburg*, and the *New York*. Unheard in these cost-conscious, efficiency-themed days, they remained at dock for five or six days between voyages. They were also noted for their midnight sailings. A nautically suited German band on deck was part of the bon voyage festivities. North German Lloyd, a sort of sister company, but based at Bremen, subleased starting in 1934. One of their ships, the *Berlin*, made headlines when she loaded American scrap metal from barges at Pier 84 and then sailed for Hitler's Germany without passengers. Disturbing bold-letter headlines included "American Metals Going to Nazi Factories!" In August 1939, just as the war was about to start, the superliner *Bremen*, moored across the slip at adjacent Pier 86, was allowed to sail for home waters, but without passengers and with carefully inspected cargoes. As tugs righted

the 51,000-ton flagship of the German Merchant Fleet, many of her 900 crewmembers took to the decks and gave the raised-arm Nazi salute as she sailed off.

Troopships came and went at Pier 84 at the height of the Second World War and then, with the Germans all but out of the shipping business for some time to come, the lease went to the American Export Lines and to a slowly reawakening firm they then represented in the United States, the Italian Line. There was the *La Guardia*, the *Saturnia*, the *Vulcania*, the *Conte Biancamano* and, beginning in 1951, the sparkling new and innovative sisters *Independence* and *Constitution*. Large and luxurious and very advanced, they were notably the first fully air-conditioned large liners to be built. The Italians, by then moving out on their own, responded with two bigger liners, the 29,000-ton *Andrea Doria* and her twin, the *Cristoforo Colombo*, between 1953 and '54. The *Doria* was, of course, due at Pier 84 on the morning of July 26, 1956, but never appeared. Instead, on that same morning, she rolled over and sank some 60 miles south of Nantucket after a collision the night before with the Swedish liner *Stockholm*. Freight and passenger luggage had already reached Pier 84 for the *Doria*'s next scheduled outward sailing on July 27, a trip she would never make. Another Italian liner, the *Conte Grande*, normally on Italian Line's Italy–South America run, was hurriedly reassigned to New York service and visits to Pier 84 to fill the void.

Later, on a hazy summer's morning in 1960, the *Doria*'s official replacement arrived, the superb *Leonardo da Vinci*. Italy's newest and finest liner to date, it was said that she hinted at the future of ocean liner design: in five years, it was planned, she would be converted to nuclear propulsion. But in reality, the arrival of commercial jets just before, in 1958, created an unbeatable rival and so the Atlantic liners were completely and utterly doomed, and like the dinosaurs, gradually slipping off into oblivion. The scrapyards were often their final destinations.

Pier 84 welcomed its last liners in the early 1970s and, with an added outer end for even larger ships, handled the likes of the 1,035-foot-long *France*, the longest liner of her day. The seven long piers that were once known as Luxury Liner Row, which included Pier 84, would be consolidated as a very seasonal, three-pier cruise terminal by 1974. Piers 88, 90, and 92 were reconstructed while others like 84 were closed and partially demolished. It was all part of the changes ahead for the great Port of New York.

When the Port Authority of New York & New Jersey, the bistate agency that controlled much of the port and its activities, bought marshlands over in Newark, New Jersey in the 1920s, they could not have imagined that it would one day become a huge container-cargo port. But containers would come later, in the mid-1950s. Newly created Pan-Atlantic Steamship Company, later rechristened Sea-Land Corporation, commissioned the world's first containership, the 10,000-ton converted tanker *Ideal X.* She had her debut in April 1956, taking on 58 truck trailers at the Marsh Street pier at Port Newark. It revolutionized cargo handling from then on. Confident, the company went on to convert existing freighters into what were initially dubbed "trailer ships," wartime-built vessels such as the *Gateway City, Azalea City, Beauregard, Raphael Semmes,* and the *Bienville,* shown here *(above)* while passing under the Verrazano-Narrows Bridge. "It is interesting to compare that ships such as the *Bienville,* the first containerships in ways, carried up to 226 containers in all. Today, there are barges that carry 1,000 containers and ships that can transport almost 10,000 at a time," added Captain McNamara. Sea-Land merged with Denmark's Maersk Line, and known as Maersk–Sea Land is today the largest containership operator in the world.

Containers, also known as "boxes," posed some initial problems. Onboard cranes, for example, were added to the earliest ships since dockside cranes had not yet been developed. The onboard equipment also allowed containerships to visit almost any port in the world. By the 1970s, however, areas such as Port Elizabeth, Staten Island, Bayonne, and Brooklyn had clusters of tall, birdlike container cranes that could load or off-load containers at the rate of 60 per hour (*left*).

Initially, in the 1960s and '70s, many cargo ships such as this vessel (*below*) belonging to the Polish Ocean Lines and berthed at Port Elizabeth were combinations of traditional break-bulk and container transport.

Containerships have grown considerably in size, with some New York–routed ships carrying well over 6,000 "boxes." At 75,000 tons and the size of, say, the *Queen Elizabeth 2*, ships such as Maersk Line's *Leda Maersk*, seen here (*opposite, top*) departing from Port Elizabeth, equal as many as eight freighters of fifty years earlier.

Pleasure boating has grown considerably in the waters in and around New York harbor. Perhaps the greatest starting point was the hugely successful Operation Sail '76, when 1,000 craft, including some of the world's great sailing ships, put into port for July 4, 1976—the bicentennial of America (*opposite, bottom*).

Ship christenings were traditionally done at shipyards, usually on the day of launching, but these nautical baptisms began to change when Princess Grace of Monaco named the brand-new liner *Cunard Princess* at New York's Pier 88 in March 1977 *(above)*. A long list of ship namings, usually involving a well-known celebrity, have since occurred at port docksides.

In its day, it welcomed the likes of Atlantic ocean liners belonging to the Anchor Line and later roving freighters from the States Marine Lines and ships on the "whiskey run" from Glasgow that sailed for Cunard. But by the late 1960s, Pier 51, located at the foot of Jane Street in Greenwich Village, was without a tenant and had fallen on hard times. By the time this photo *(below)* was taken in September 1977, docks such as this were unsightly reminders of a largely bygone era along much of the port's waterfront.

One pier with great history stood until as late as 1993. Located at the foot of West 14th Street, 1907-built Pier 56 *(opposite, top)* was part of the great Chelsea Docks, a series of finger piers that, until the mid-1930s, handled some of the greatest of Atlantic liners, ships such as the *Mauretania, Olympic, Aquitania, Berengaria, Ile de France,* and *Rex.* But it was at Pier 56, in April 1912 that the 705 survivors of the ill-fated *Titanic* landed in New York. The heroic rescue ship was an otherwise small, insignificant Cunarder, the *Carpathia.*

While replaced by the likes of Florida's Miami and Port Everglades, and even San Juan, Puerto Rico, all of which have greater passenger ship traffic, the lull that seemed to overtake New York as a liner port ended in the late 1990s. Increasingly, more, as well as larger ships came to call, at least in the peak cruise season months between May and October. By 2004, figures soared to over 700,000 passengers. Here *(opposite, bottom),* in this 2001 photograph, we see one of the world's largest liners, the 101,000-ton "floating resort" *Carnival Triumph.* Carrying up to 3,100 passengers, she sailed on continuous short cruises from Manhattan's West Side to the likes of Bermuda, Halifax, and Portland, Maine. By 2004, Carnival, the largest cruise operator in the world, had three mega-liners sailing from New York.

A high point in New York harbor history came on Sunday, April 25, 2004. The popular, 1969-commissioned, 70,000-ton *Queen Elizabeth 2* arrived at Pier 90 and met her successor of sorts, the brand-new, 148,000-ton *Queen Mary 2*, the largest liner yet built, for the first time *(above)*. That night, surrounded by tugs, spectator and pleasure craft, and, of course, spurting fireboats, the two superliners sailed simultaneously, but then paused for a gala, celebratory fireworks display off the Statue of Liberty. It was a grand celebration of Cunard, the great liners, the two "Queens" and, most fittingly, the great Port of New York.

Afterword

New York harbor is indeed a magical place. On a Saturday morning in early June 2004, the setting was superb. The city's weather was flawless. The skies overhead were ink blue, the light soft and clear, the visibility crystalline and seemingly limitless. You could almost see all the way to Portugal!

We were fortunate: a boat ride was in our schedule. On a chartered craft with several hundred fellow guests aboard, our journey had, in fact, a very specific purpose: the 100th anniversary of the tragic burning and near-sinking of the steamer *General Slocum*. Some 957 perished in the churning, Long Island Sound waters just north of Hell Gate. Once at the site, there were commemorative speeches, a narrative, and the tossing of wreaths and carnations. A clergyman added a blessing while several surrounding boats paused in momentary vigil as a city fireboat elegantly sprayed great hoops of colored water. Whistles then sounded in rightful homage, followed by a deep silence. Those lost souls were fittingly remembered.

We had undocked from Lower Manhattan, from the piers of South Street Seaport Museum and where, decades before, passenger ships, tramp steamers, and those ever-romantic banana boats had cast off for the likes of Havana, Vera Cruz, and Cartagena. An immortal ship, the liner *Morro Castle*, which hideously burned off the New Jersey shore in September 1934 with the loss of 122 passengers and crew, used nearby Pier 15, one dock to the north. Our boat swung out and then turned north, eventually moving along the mighty East River and under that trio of illustrious bridges: the Brooklyn, the Manhattan, and the Williamsburg.

While Manhattan's cityscape is dominated by those great skyscrapers, the opposite Brooklyn shore is lower, gentler, perhaps less inhibiting and more individualistic. There, in melancholy splendor, also sat the great warehouses, factories, and piers that once pulsated, hummed and drummed, and churned with commerce and trade and, of course, shipping. I thought back to those busier times, to the 1950s and '60s, when those very docks were crammed with freighters, their matchstick-like booms swung in every direction, loading and off-loading freight of every kind and type, and from the far corners of the earth: Capetown, Hamburg, Yokohama, Valparaiso, and Trinidad. There was the Meyer Line, Farrell Lines, Moore-McCormack Lines, Grancolombiana, the Elder Dempster Lines, NYK Line, and the Barber Line. And they were the names belonging to just the upper-Brooklyn docks. Dozens and dozens were left to the lower Brooklyn waterfront, extending southward to the mammoth Army Terminal down at 58th Street.

"I even loved the smells of those old Brooklyn docks. There were the smells of the hemp lines, the smells of the combinations of the oils and the greases, the smells of our cargoes, the smells of the wood pilings and, of course, the smells of the river itself," remembered Captain Dag Dvergastein, present-day master of an ultra-luxurious cruise ship, the *Seven Seas Voyager*. Then, however, the young Dag was a junior on Norwegian-flag, Barber Line freighters. Barber was actually the American agent's name. The ships belonged to the Oslo-based Wilhelmsen Lines, and possibly best remembered for their impeccable freighters, which all had names that began with the letter "T." Dag served aboard the likes of the *Taronga, Tegola, Trianon, Tennessee,* and *Taiping*. "We would lay over in the Brooklyn docks for days at a time, usually a full week in fact, off-loading and then reloading for the next voyage. It all took much longer, even in the 1970s, as the changeover to full containers was not yet complete. I often did the night watch onboard, sometimes casting a glance backward at the great Manhattan skyline, those towers glowing and reaching for the sky. The combination of ship, pier, cargo, and the city was fascinating, intoxicating, absolute poetry."

The Barber Line freighters carried an enormous range of freight in their six, seven, even eight holds. "We were like 'floating supermarkets,'" noted the Captain. "We would have mail, shirts, California apples, steel, bourbon, bags of corn, and American-made cars encased in plywood. We'd also have toys from Taiwan, automobile parts from Japan, bed sheets from China, latex and tapioca from Bangkok, and yet other items such as canned sardines, fireworks, clocks, and construction equipment. We had a very organized routing in those days, from Brooklyn to the Panama Canal and the West Coast before heading for the Far East. Afterward, we would return from the East again through Panama and stopping in the Caribbean before calling at a succession of U.S. ports before returning to Brooklyn. The full voyage took as long as four or five months."

But as more efficient containerization took hold in the 1980s, the steamship tenants left the Brooklyn docks for the wider, more expansive docklands at Port Elizabeth in New Jersey. The Brooklyn waterfront, once teeming with ships and maritime activity, grew desolate, lonely, decrepit, steadily decaying. By 2004, there were all sorts of revivalist plans: parklands, hotels, shopping malls, and, of course, luxury apartments. There was even a short-lived scheme to bring the idle superliner *United States* to the Fulton Street Pier and moor her there as a museum, tourist attraction, and indeed a new landmark to the Brooklyn waterfront. That plan never came to pass, sadly.

As our boat sailed along the East River on that more recent Saturday morning, I often thought back, in seeing those melancholy docks and warehouses and the other waterside remains, of what was a very different, but now bygone era in otherwise glorious New York harbor.

Bibliography

Braynard, Frank O. & Miller, William H. *Fifty Famous Liners*, Volumes 1–3. Cambridge, England: Patrick Stephens Limited, 1982–86.

Bunker, John W. *Harbor & Haven: An Illustrated History of the Port of New York*. Woodland Hills, California: Windsor Publications, Inc., 1979.

Devol, George & Cassidy, Tom (editors). *Ocean & Cruise News* (1980–2004). Stamford, Connecticut: World Ocean & Cruise Society.

Duffy, Francis J. & Miller, William H. *The New York Harbor Book*. Falmouth, Maine: TBW Books, 1986.

Kludas, Arnold. *Great Passenger Ships of the World*, Volumes 1–5. Cambridge, England: Patrick Stephens Limited, 1972–76.

Miller, William H. *New York Shipping*. London: Carmania Press Limited, 1994.

Moody, Bert. *Ocean Ships*. London: Ian Allan Limited, 1959–71.

New York Port Handbook. New York: Port Resources Information Committee, Inc., 1958–64.

Official Steamship Guide. New York: Transportation Guides Inc., 1937–63.

Sawyer, L. A. & Mitchell, W. H. *The Liberty Ships*. Newton Abbot, Devon: David & Charles Limited, 1973.

Ships & Sailing. Milwaukee, Wisconsin: Kalmbach Publishing Co., 1950–60.

Steamboat Bill. New York: Steamship Historical Society of America, Inc., 1966–2004.

Towline. New York: Moran Towing & Transportation Company, 1950–98.

Index of Ships